NEW DIRECTIONS FOR ADULT AN[...]

Ralph G. Brockett, *University of Tenn[...]*
EDITOR-IN-CHIEF

Alan B. Knox, *University of Wisconsin, Madison*
CONSULTING EDITOR

Applying Cognitive Learning Theory to Adult Learning

Daniele D. Flannery
The Pennsylvania State University

EDITOR

Number 59, Fall 1993

JOSSEY-BASS PUBLISHERS
San Francisco

APPLYING COGNITIVE LEARNING THEORY TO ADULT LEARNING
Daniele D. Flannery (ed.)
New Directions for Adult and Continuing Education, no. 59
Ralph G. Brockett, Editor-in-Chief
Alan B. Knox, Consulting Editor

Microfilm copies of issues and articles are available in 16mm and 35mm,
as well as microfiche in 105mm, through University Microfilms Inc., 300
North Zeeb Road, Ann Arbor, Michigan 48106-1346.

LC 85-644750   ISSN 0195-2242   ISBN 1-55542-716-2

NEW DIRECTIONS FOR ADULT AND CONTINUING EDUCATION is part of The
Jossey-Bass Higher and Adult Education Series and is published quarterly
by Jossey-Bass Inc., Publishers, 350 Sansome Street, San Francisco,
California 94104-1310 (publication number USPS 493-930). Second-class
postage paid at San Francisco, California, and at additional mailing offices.
POSTMASTER: Send address changes to New Directions for Adult and
Continuing Education, Jossey-Bass Inc., Publishers, 350 Sansome Street,
San Francisco, California 94104-1310.

SUBSCRIPTIONS for 1993 cost $47.00 for individuals and $62.00 for institutions, agencies, and libraries.

EDITORIAL CORRESPONDENCE should be sent to the Editor-in-Chief, Ralph
G. Brockett, Department of Educational Leadership, University of Tennessee, 239 Claxton Addition, Knoxville, Tennessee 37996-3400.

Cover photograph by Wernher Krutein/PHOTOVAULT © 1990.

The paper used in this journal is acid-free and meets the strictest
guidelines in the United States for recycled paper (50 percent
recycled waste, including 10 percent postconsumer waste). Manu-
factured in the United States of America.

CONTENTS

Editor's Notes

Successful learning for adults is the key to becoming literate, to maintaining workplace skills, and to participating in continued development as individuals and world citizens. Not only is there an unprecedented increase in the demand for adult learning opportunities, but the learners to whom learning opportunities must be directed are increasingly diverse. One way this diversity expresses itself is in the variety of cognitive learning strategies adults bring to the teaching-learning exchange. These strategies influence adults' abilities to acquire, process, store, and retrieve the information presented in the instruction or program. Research demonstrates that certain strategies are more effective than others in formal learning settings. At minimum, successful adult learning depends on having the learning strategies to acquire the desired knowledge or skills. For example, in literacy training, people must have the strategies that match those of the texts and programs they are utilizing and on which they will be tested, or they are not likely to be successful. Adult graduate students must have the cognitive learning strategies to think and write analytically, or they will not be able to complete a thesis or dissertation project. Furthermore, adults' cognitive strategies give them the necessary foundation for engaging in Knowles's andragogy and Mezirow's perspective transformation. Regrettably, basic cognitive learning theory has often been slighted in adult learning courses or has been assumed to be so rudimentary that it is missing entirely. Yet an understanding of it is a prerequisite to facilitating successful learning.

The chapters in this volume are intended to assist instructors, program planners, continuing educators, and trainers in the process of facilitating successful learning through knowledge of and use of basic cognitive learning theory.

Cognition refers to the way an individual experiences, processes, organizes, stores, and retrieves information. Cognitive styles, or cognitive learning styles, are "information processing habits representing the learner's typical mode of perceiving, thinking, problem solving, and remembering" (Messick and Associates, 1976, p. 13). Cognitive styles differ, since each learner has preferred ways of processing information. Furthermore, learners may adapt their typical ways of information processing to meet the needs of the teacher, the subject matter, and the classroom structure. The term *cognitive strategies* used in this book denotes the way a learner goes about learning in a particular context. This may or may not be the learner's typical cognitive style (Das, 1988). Chapters One and Two concentrate on two dimensions of cognitive style—perceptual modality preferences and global and analytical ways of experiencing and processing information, respectively. These chapters describe the particular characteristics of each dimension, ways of iden-

New Directions for Adult and Continuing Education, no. 59, Fall 1993   © Jossey-Bass Publishers

tifying the cognitive strategies in learners' behavior, and methods of presentation that may facilitate or inhibit learning by people with each of the cognitive characteristics.

While not the focus of this sourcebook, the affective cannot be separated from the cognitive dimension, since the emotions are involved in every aspect of learning. The term *affective* refers to those aspects of personality having to do with attention, emotion, and valuing. *Affective styles* are those typical ways of responding to or desiring a need for structure, curiosity, persistence or perseverance, levels of anxiety, frustration tolerance, locus of control, achievement motivation, self-actualization, imitation, risk taking, competition, cooperation, level of aspiration, reaction to reinforcement, social motivation, and personal interests (Messick and Associates, 1976). Chapter Three introduces the affective domain, considers the integral connection between cognitive and affective processing in learning, and offers strategies for enhancing the affective dimension in learning environments.

Chapter Four presents a discussion of the functions of memory and offers suggestions for enhancing the retention and recall of learning. Further, this chapter considers the relationship of memory to perceptual modalities, to global and analytical ways of processing information, and to the affective dimension.

In the later chapters, the focus moves to broader issues related to basic cognitive theory in adult learning. Chapter Five provides basic guidelines for considering the use of learning-style instruments. Learning styles are defined broadly to include cognitive, affective, and physiological styles. A new, thorough review and critique of available adult learning-style instruments concerned with perceptual modalities is offered.

Finally, it is not enough to consider applying learning theory within formal instructional processes alone. All learning is not transferable to each and every learning setting (Lave, 1988). Rather, the experiences and exchanges within each setting influence the ways people go about learning and their success at it. Therefore, if they are to take control of their own learning, adult learners must be purposively taught not only how to engage in learning, but also how to successfully engage in learning in real-world settings. Chapter Six introduces the concept of learning how to learn and suggests how learning to learn can be incorporated into various types of teaching-learning exchanges.

Following up on the content of Chapter Six, Chapter Seven presents one aspect of learning how to learn: the cognitive apprenticeship approach to learning and teaching, in which experts model how to think about the solutions to problems situated in everyday professional practice.

Chapter Eight summarizes the themes of the sourcebook and offers further sources for understanding the influence of social and cultural context on adults as learners.

Each of the collaborators in this sourcebook project wishes you success as you join us in the journey toward understanding the importance of cognitive learning theory and in actively working to apply it in our teaching-learning exchanges. Remember, what we are about as adult educators, regardless of the setting, is facilitating successful learning.

Daniele D. Flannery
Editor

References

Das, J. P. "Simultaneous-Successive Processing and Planning: Implications for School Learning." In R. Schmeck (ed.), *Learning Strategies and Learning Styles.* New York: Plenum Press, 1988.

Lave, J. *Cognition in Practice: Mind, Mathematics and Culture in Everyday Life.* Cambridge, England: Cambridge University Press, 1988.

Messick, S., and Associates. *Individuality in Learning: Implications of Cognitive Styles and Creativity for Human Development.* San Francisco: Jossey-Bass, 1976.

DANIÈLE D. FLANNERY is assistant professor of adult education and coordinator of the adult education Doctor of Education program at The Pennsylvania State University, Harrisburg.

Building on learners' perceptual modalities facilitates learning.

What Are Perceptual Modalities and How Do They Contribute to Learning?

Robert F. Wislock

Perceptual modalities are critically important aspects of cognition to attend to in educating adults (James and Galbraith, 1985). A perceptual modality can be defined as the means through which information is extracted from the environment (James and Galbraith, 1985). Similarly, Messick and Associates (1976) describe perceptual modalities as individual consistencies in relative degree of reliance on the different sensory modalities available for experiencing the world. Perceptual modalities "provide a means for potentially reaching every learner and for making the quality of the instructional learning process more effective. . . . If adult learners are encouraged to utilize their dominant perceptual learning modality, the learners will be more successful in their learning endeavors whether it be in the classroom or in self-directed inquiry" (James and Galbraith, p. 20).

The purpose of this chapter is to examine the concept of perceptual modality and its implications for the practitioner in the development and facilitation of programs.

Perceptual Modalities

The brain receives information in a learning setting through a network of perceptual modalities. This information is the raw data that the brain processes for learning to occur. Individuals receive this information in three ways: visual, which is viewing and reading; aural, which is hearing and speaking; and psychomotor, which is doing. James and Galbraith (1985) expand the list of modalities to seven elements: print, in which individuals learn by reading and writing; aural, which focuses on listening to other individuals and ourselves, through lectures, audiotapes, or reading aloud to oneself; interactive, which is discussing ideas in groups or by debate activities; visual, which may be individuals observing videos, graphs, words, or pictures; haptic, which is the sense of touch by hands-on experience; kinesthetic, in which participants learn while engaged in physical movement such as taking notes or pacing; and olfactory, which involves the sense of smell.

Adult learners differ in the perceptual modalities that they prefer to use in processing information. A dominant preference may form early in life and not change radically (Keefe, 1988). This preferred reliance on one of the sensory modes is called the individual's *dominant modality*. It is the sensory channel through which information is processed most efficiently. Several modalities can also function in parallel with one another, with information from one clarifying and supplementing information from the other modalities. A modality that clarifies or supplements information from the other modalities is described as a *secondary modality*. This modality enhances rather than interferes with the functioning of the dominant modality. For some individuals, learning strengths may reside equally in several perceptual modalities and not just in one dominant modality. When two or more sensory channels are equally efficient, the result is referred to as a *mixed modality strength*. Often as adults mature, "their modalities become integrated as they discover cognitive structures to transfer information from one modality to another. . . . But when a situation is stressful or when the consequences of an event are important, adults will tend to resort to their dominant modality" (Barbe and Swassing, 1988, p. 6).

This perceptual sensory network, which is unique to the individual learner, provides important information to the brain, which must process the data if learning is to occur. If a deficit exists in one modality, the brain will receive incomplete data and limited learning may occur. The same situation can occur if the data are not presented in a clear fashion or if the learner does not attend to the information. Therefore, the critical issue becomes, How can the adult educator integrate an individual's perceptual modality in instructional design or in facilitating learning?

Determining One's Perceptual Modality

Modality-based instruction is one approach that focuses on learning and perceptual modalities. Proponents describe this as a comprehensive approach grounded in the assumption that facilitation and program planning should be organized around a participant's strongest modality. Developing an awareness of the educator's and participants' modalities is an initial strategy in the modality-based instruction process. In fact, "it is the most important strategy because it is a frame of mind that guides the facilitator in curriculum development and instruction" (Barbe and Swassing, 1988, p. 14). This awareness is important since facilitators may project their own modality strengths into the selection of materials as well as into teaching strategies and processes. For example, instructors who rely on the visual modality may consistently select and use videos, overheads, and similar methods in their instructional approaches. The instructors in this situation may neglect the needs of learners whose strengths are in the auditory or kinesthetic modalities. Basically, this self-awareness can help instructors adapt their instructional styles to accommodate participants with modality strengths different from the facilitators' strengths. In a study of public school teachers, Barbe and Milone (1980) discovered that they preferred the visual modality for their own learning and teaching. The least preferred modality was kinesthetic. The study concluded that the overwhelming rejection of the kinesthetic modality may suggest that certain students can be aided or handicapped by educators' teaching-learning preferences. By socializing learners away from the kinesthetic modality, this situation could have critical implications for later learning contexts in which participants are required to assemble objects or use hands-on experience with different types of equipment. Barbe and Milone stress the importance of developing this awareness by stating that as educators, "we teach as we learn best, not as we were taught" (p. 44).

Facilitators must also become aware of the participants' perceptual modalities. This awareness will aid facilitators in selecting diverse materials and methods to individualize the instruction to meet the learners' needs. In a literature review, Harter (1981) found that the studies indicated that from kindergarten to sixth grade, vision seems to be the strongest modality, kinesthetic next, and audition last. From the late elementary grades to adulthood, vision remained the dominant modality, with audition second and kinesthetic learning least important. In their study of adult perceptual modalities, James and Galbraith (1985) also found that individuals between twenty and forty-nine years of age preferred the visual modality. However, their study found that haptic was second; interactive, third; and aural, fourth. For persons fifty years and over, visual remained first, but interactive moved to second, followed by aural and haptic.

Both facilitators and participants can discover their perceptual modalities in several ways. First, a modality can be described as a preference. This assessment reflects individuals' personal opinions concerning the modality through which they learn best. The source of information is the individual learner. James and Galbraith (1985) identify the Perceptual Learning Style Inventory and the Multi Modal Paired Associates Learning Test–Revised as two instruments that practitioners or learners can use to become aware of their modality preferences (see Chapter Five for more information on these inventories).

Another way of discovering learners' modality preferences is through the personal interview. Educators ask learners questions to identify the strong and weak elements of their individual modalities. (See James and Galbraith, 1985, p. 23, for a list of questions that educators can use in the interview process.) Both of these assessment methods measure learners' preferences. Advocates of these methods believe that learners themselves are the best judges of their needs and interests. However, other educators, such as Barbe and Swassing (1988), criticize these methods. They suggest that personal preference may not be reliable, since most individuals are not trained observers of their behaviors. In addition, learners may respond in a socially accepted manner when asked about their modality preferences.

A third major way to assess an individual's perceptual modality is to view it as a measurable behavior. In this assessment context, a modality strength is defined as an individual's ability to perform an academically relevant task in each of the major modalities. According to Swassing and Barbe (1988), this approach acknowledges that a preference exists that can be described as the most comfortable way of receiving information, but it is not always consistent with the way information is most efficiently received and processed. The Swassing-Barbe Modality Index is one instrument that measures modality strength (see Chapter Five for more details on this instrument). The individual is presented with a variety of stimuli in each of the modalities. The strongest modality is the one in which the task is completed most efficiently (Barbe and Swassing, 1988). Dunn (1988), who is a critic of this method, questions Barbe and Swassing's contention of whether a preference is really a strength. She characterizes it as "a question of dichotomizing between pleasure and pain. If you like it, perhaps it isn't good for you; perhaps a little pain will be more productive" (p. 305). James and Galbraith (1985) also criticize this approach because these instruments are complex to administer and interpret.

Several other innovative methods can also be used to assess an individual's perceptual modalities. Bandler and Grinder (1979) note that individuals move their eyes in systematic directions as they process information. These systematic movements are called *eye processing cues*. People who look up when accessing information are likely to process information visually. People who look down are likely to process information kinesthetically. People who look horizontally are likely to process information auditorially. A second method focuses on the "predicates," or basic words, that individuals emphasize in their conversations with adult educators. For example, if learners frequently use phrases like "it appears to me," "it looks to me," and "as I see it" during the assessment interaction, they tend to process information visually. This assessment device also indicates whether individuals use their auditory or kinesthetic perceptual modalities in the learning process.

Researchers and practitioners who are proponents of modality-based instruction believe that an initial strategy in this approach is to develop an awareness of individuals' perceptual modalities. This "frame of mind" will help guide the instructor or planner in the selection and use of instructional methods and materials. Perceptual modalities can be viewed and assessed as preferences or as strengths. Debate centers around the methods that should be used. Practitioners should investigate these arguments before selecting a method. They must also consider other variables in this selection process. Time constraints, resource allocations, and the learners themselves are a few important elements to be reviewed in this process. Future research about the assessment methods can also help the educator in developing a better understanding of these methods.

Possible Instructional Approaches

As practitioners critically review this important information about learners' perceptual modalities, they can begin to design and implement programs based on individual needs. Advocates of modality-based instruction propose two major strategies. The first strategy is the use of the multisensory approach. In this approach, the facilitator uses a variety of teaching processes, activities, and materials to meet the adults' diverse perceptual modalities. A specific example of how an educator can apply the multisensory approach involves the facilitation of a fire safety program at Bloomsburg University in Bloomsburg, Pennsylvania. The program's focus is to teach employees how to react if a fire occurs and how to use an extinguisher. This approach draws on various methods to meet the participants' modalities. The aural and print modalities are stimulated by a lecture on the different types of fires, the types of extinguishers available, and the criteria one should use in deciding to fight a fire. This verbal information is reinforced by overheads that highlight the key points. A video—a visual element—is shown to summarize the topic. An interactive discussion follows to review the various fire situations and the participants' reactions. Employees then participate in a hands-on exercise where they extinguish an actual fire.

Keefe (1988) believes that an adult educator's or organization's commitment to this multisensory approach can eventually move the instructional process from the use of a variety of methods and materials in an entire program, as in the fire safety program, to a more individualized approach. James and Blank (1991) explain that in the more individualized type of instructional approach, a primary step in the development and facilitation of a program is to determine the preferred learning styles of groups of adults with similar characteristics. Instruction can then be tailored to each group, instead of a comprehensive approach being used for the entire group. In the fire safety example, participants with visual strengths might be involved with interactive video programs, individuals with interactive preferences would work in discussion groups, and participants with kinesthetic tendencies might handle the actual materials on the job. In this learning setting, the participants' perceptual modality profiles are used to develop several individualized strategies to achieve common program objectives.

In the management development program at Bloomsburg University, supervisors' and directors' perceptual modalities are assessed using the Multi

Modal Paired Associates Learning Test–Revised. Based on these data, the training manager assigns participants to learning groups emphasizing the appropriate modalities. Although the program topic is the same for the groups, different learning methods are used to match the group's primary perceptual modality so the participants can master the content. For example, in an effective decision-making program, kinesthetic learners use in-basket exercises. They make decisions about work assignments and process the materials from the in-basket until all the appropriate work assignments are physically placed in the out-basket. This exercise emphasizes motion from one basket to another similar to an individual pacing or taking notes during a learning interaction. The physical motion aids the learning process. Similarly, in a group of managers that rely on the interactive perceptual modality, a case-study approach is utilized in the instructional process. Small groups of supervisors discuss specific case studies about decision-making scenarios and recommend appropriate actions in these different situations. These learning activities rely on participation and discussion by the program participants. In this individualized approach to perceptual modalities, the learning methods are closely matched to the groups and their respective modalities. Practitioners need to explore innovative instructional methods and techniques to apply to these unique learning situations. Resources such as *Approaches to Training and Development* (Laird, 1985) can stimulate the adult educator in selecting these unique learning methods.

This strategy has been critical for four staff employees at Bloomsburg University who are unable to read the print materials in the safety education programs. Frequently, the print modality is the predominant method used by adult educators. Working with these employees individually, instructors have instead utilized kinesthetic methods that stress hands-on experiences with various safety practices concerning fire safety, lifting, and hepatitis B programs. Typically, the safety principles are described (auditory modality) through discussions, demonstrations (visual modality), and videos (visual modality). Participants then actually work with the safety materials or methods to master the content (kinesthetic modality). Throughout the process, the facilitator provides feedback to the participant, and the discussion (interactive modality) between these individuals clarifies the program content.

Evaluation—A Key Element in the Instructional Process

Few practitioners would dispute the importance of evaluation in the instructional process. An educator's philosophy of adult education and the type of program facilitated are key elements in determining the overall evaluation approach used in each learning situation—that is, mastering behavioral learning objectives or participants' achieving their own learning goals. Yet in many education and training programs, the print modality or written exams are the primary means of evaluation. This mode of evaluation may not be appropriate for all learners, especially if their primary perceptual modality differs from the type of evaluation method used. It is logical to assume that if learners receive and process the information through certain perceptual modalities, they will also demonstrate mastery of the content through the same modality. An appropriate evaluation method should promote recall of the information through the particular modalities used to initially receive this information. It is critical for the facilitator to employ evaluation methods that require a great variety of responses from the individual learner. For example, after reading a series of articles about delegating tasks, learners whose perceptual modality is visual can assess their learning progress by diagramming the major points of the articles or by drawing pictures that demonstrate these points. Interactive participants might show their knowledge of delegating tasks by demonstrating in a role play the essential steps or actions that comprise the process of effective delegation. These evaluation situations challenge practitioners to become creative in their selection of evaluation techniques and to test these methods in instructional settings with learners differing in perceptual modalities. Naturalistic observations and research studies can help build sound theory and practice with regard to effective and varied evaluation techniques.

Conclusion

Perceptual modality is defined as the means through which information is obtained from the environment or the learning setting. This information is the data that an individual's brain must process for learning to occur. Theorists believe people can receive the information in a variety of ways, which may include visual, aural, and kinesthetic strategies. The emphasis on individuals' perceptual modalities provides a means of sensitizing the educator to the needs and interests of learners.

Assessment instruments provide data about the facilitator's and the learners' perceptual modality strengths or preferences. Data about the learners' perceptual modality strengths or preferences will help the practitioner begin to design or facilitate effective programs based on individualizing the instructional processes and materials.

Proponents of modality-based instruction believe that the practitioner can use two major strategies in the learning setting to individualize instruction for the participants. The first strategy is the multisensory approach. In this strategy, the facilitator uses a variety of teaching processes and materials to meet the learner's perceptual modalities. The second strategy is the point-of-intervention approach. In this approach, participants are either grouped by their perceptual modality or directed to materials on which they can work individually after they have demonstrated difficulty in understanding the program content.

Debate and controversy surround the concept of perceptual modality.

Critics have questioned the need for this type of instruction. Some educators debate whether it is more appropriate for facilitators to adapt their instruction to the learners' perceptual modalities or whether participants should adapt to the facilitator's methods of instruction. James and Blank (1991) point out that some educators, such as Brookfield (1986), believe that introducing students to different perceptual modalities may have benefits for these learners. One benefit is that at some point in the learning experience, learners will use their preferred modality. A second benefit is that learners will be exposed to and use the other learning modalities, which will increase their adaptability in a variety of learning experiences. Another major criticism of using perceptual modality in instruction focuses on the results of research studies. After reviewing the results of earlier studies, Harter (1981) concluded that most studies found no positive relationship between matching instruction and a student's modality. A majority of these research studies have been conducted with school-age students and not adult learners. In contrast, Dunn (1988) and other researchers strongly recommend a need for further research because of various design problems in these studies. First, the instruments used in these studies to measure preferred or strongest modality are not in agreement and generally have poor reliability and validity. (See Chapter Five for a discussion of reliability and validity.) Second, researchers tend to examine group findings, which may not be a valid way to determine whether individuals achieve better in comparison with their own baseline data when taught through strengths or preferences.

To resolve these problems, Dunn (1988, pp. 304–305) feels "future research needs to compare how each learner with identified preferences achieves with visual, auditory, and kinesthetic resources and how those treatments affect their attitudes and self confidence. . . . The research needs to look at individuals, not groups; and use reliable instruments to detect relative strengths of the modalities in those individuals." Martini (1986) and Kroon (1985) have incorporated these suggestions in their research on perceptual modalities. Both studies have demonstrated a positive relationship between teaching in an individual's perceptual modality and an increase in the individual's achievement level. These studies were conducted with high school students. There is also a need for more systematic research on perceptual modalities in the adult education field, where this kind of research is almost nonexistent.

These findings reveal a need for refined research designs in investigating perceptual modalities and exploring their use in program planning and facilitation. The adult educator will come to a better understanding of the role perceptual modalities can play in the learning setting through research as well as by using and evaluating the instructional approaches in actual learning settings. As James and Galbraith (1988, p. 22) emphasize, "Research and practice can serve as focal points for further development and investigation of the concept of perceptual modalities."

References

Bandler, R., and Grinder, J. *Frogs into Princes*. Moab, Utah: Real People Press, 1979.

Barbe, W. B., and Milone, M. N., Jr. "Modality." *Instructor*, 1980, *89*, 44–47.

Barbe, W. B., and Swassing, R. H. *Teaching Through Modality Strengths: Concepts and Practices*. Columbus, Ohio: Zaner-Bloser, 1988.

Brookfield, S. D. *Understanding and Facilitating Adult Learning: A Comprehensive Analysis of Principles and Effective Practices*. San Francisco: Jossey-Bass, 1986.

Dunn, R. "Teaching Students Through Their Perceptual Strengths or Preferences." *Journal of Reading*, 1988, *31*, 304–309.

Harter, N. *Swassing/Barbe Index Applied to Selected Students*. Alexandria, Va.: ERIC Clearinghouse, 1981.

James, W. B., and Blank, W. E. "A Comparison of Perceptual Learning Styles of Adult High School Graduates and Nongraduates." *Adult Basic Education*, 1991, *1*, 98–106.

James, W. B., and Galbraith, M. W. "Perceptual Learning Styles: Implications and Techniques for the Practitioner." *Lifelong Learning*, 1985, *8*, 20–23.

Keefe, J. W. *Profiling and Utilizing Learning Style*. Reston, Va.: National Association of Secondary School Principals, 1988.

Kroon, D. K. "An Experimental Investigation of the Effects on Academic Achievement and the Resultant Administrative Implications of Instruction Congruent and Incongruent with Students' Learning Style Perceptual Preferences." Unpublished doctoral dissertation, School of Education, St. John's University, Jamaica, N.Y., 1985.

Laird, D. *Approaches to Training and Development*. Reading, Mass.: Addison-Wesley, 1985.

Martini, M. "An Analysis of the Relationships Between and Among Computer Assisted Instruction, Learning Style Perceptual Preferences, Attitudes, and Achievement." Unpublished doctoral dissertation, School of Education, St. John's University, Jamaica, N.Y., 1986.

Messick, S., and Associates. *Individuality in Learning: Implications of Cognitive Styles and Creativity for Human Development*. San Francisco: Jossey-Bass, 1976.

Papalia, D. C., and Olds, S. W. *Human Development*. New York: McGraw-Hill, 1979.

ROBERT F. WISLOCK *is director of training and education at Bloomsburg University, Bloomsburg, Pennsylvania.*

To be a successful learner in the twenty-first century, one must be adept at processing information both globally and analytically.

Global and Analytical Ways of Processing Information

Daniele D. Flannery

Just before the beginning of a training session, two participants are asked, "What is the best way for the trainer to begin the session for you?" Eric replies that he would like the trainer to give a broad overview of what the session will be about. Felicia says she would like the trainer to present a detailed outline of the session to come.

This scenario is about two people who process information differently. In Chapter One, the emphasis was on processing information through perceptual modalities. This chapter will look at information processing using two cognitive styles, global and analytical. Eric processes information in a more global manner, taking in the gist of what is to occur. Felicia processes information in a more analytical manner, asking that the session be broken down into component parts in an outline format. These differences represent an important aspect of their cognitive learning styles. People concerned with the teaching-learning exchange must understand analytical and global ways of processing information. They represent qualitatively different ways of perceiving and experiencing the environment and of encoding, storing, and retrieving information from the memory. Analytical and global ways of processing information have also been related to success or failure in learning settings (Cawley, Miller, and Milligan, 1976; Cranston and McCort, 1985; Flannery, 1991; Schmeck, 1988; Smith, 1982; Witkin, Moore, Goodenough, and Cox, 1977).

This chapter will look briefly at analytical and global cognitive learning styles (see Chapter Five for more on learning styles), discuss how to identify analytical and global cognitive learning styles, and offer ideas for teaching analytical and global learners.

New Directions for Adult and Continuing Education, no. 59, Fall 1993   © Jossey-Bass Publishers

Concepts of Analytical and Global Information Processing

Analytical and global constructs of information processing are present in the literatures of three separate but related fields: cognitive psychology (Cohen, 1969), hemisphericity (Herrmann, 1990; Levy, 1974; Luria, 1973; Ornstein, 1972), and field articulation (Witkin, Moore, Goodenough, and Cox, 1977). Cognitive psychology uses the terms *analytical* and *global,* the hemisphericity literature uses *right brain* and *left brain,* and the articulation literature uses *field independent* and *field dependent* (or *field sensitive*). Whatever the terms used, these literatures cite similar characteristics for the learners. Learners who are referred to as analytical, left brained, and field independent share many of the same characteristics. Similarly, learners who are referred to as global, right brained, and field dependent share many of the same characteristics.

What are the characteristics of global information processors? To make sense of the world in a global manner is to take in the whole picture—to get a summary or gist of things. Eric wanted an overview of the training session. Global learners process information in a simultaneous manner. The ideas or experiences are seen all at once, not in any observable order. Global information processors take in information in a subjective and concrete manner. Information must be connected to what people value in their own subjective worlds. If it does not connect to what is personal, it is discarded as unimportant. The concrete aspect refers to the information or experience about real things. Otherwise, the learner cannot get a grasp of the information.

The characteristics of analytical information processors are different. To take in the world analytically is to take in the discrete details of a picture. Felicia asked for a specific outline of the important points the training session would cover. Analytical learners process information in a step-by-step manner, often in a logical way. They perceive information in an objective and abstract manner. For analytical learners, the information need not be connected to the personal experience of the processor, nor does it need to be concrete.

To understand the connection of global and analytical processing to the teaching-learning exchange, it is necessary to look at learners and the learning settings. Teachers, texts, and learning structures are included in the concept of learning settings.

There are individual differences in learners' analytical and global learning styles. Some learners are either very analytical or very global in the way they process all information. Other learners possess some information processing strengths that are analytical and some that are global; they may also have information processing weaknesses from each style. Yet other learners—holistic learners—have most of the global and analytical characteristics and demonstrate these as learning strategies when needed. Some learners are consistent in the ways they process information in teaching-learning settings.

Others have learned to adapt analytical or global strategies to those called for by the learning situation.

Teaching-learning settings vary in their demand for global or analytical processing. Teachers and tutors have their own ways of processing information; they may be more global or more analytical. Most often, teachers teach the way they process information. So teacher A may require more global processing of information from the learners, while teacher B may require a more analytical approach. Texts, too, can be oriented more toward global or analytical information processing. Learning structures may vary in their demand for global or analytical processing. For example, training programs, university classes for returning adult students, and much literacy learning have followed a school-structured model, which is likely to favor analytical processing. Testing structures with true-false and multiple-choice questions—such as the General Equivalency Diploma (GED) and the Graduate Record Examination (GRE)—demand analytical processing, which asks for the ability to segment and dissect questions into discrete parts.

As a result, the aspects of both global and analytical information processing must be critically analyzed in the total teaching-learning exchange. More specifically, they must be looked at in regard to learners, teachers, texts, and structures. Often analytical and global information processing are portrayed as different ends of a continuum, suggesting they are polar opposites. This either-or approach has tended to suggest that an analytical approach, which many settings demand, is better than a global one. Further, this framework concentrates on the larger construct of analytical or global learning, rather than on the particular skills within those constructs that learners, teachers, settings, and texts have or need to improve. Others say the goal of the teaching-learning exchange should be to be holistic, to be able to process information both ways. The holistic approach is a plausible alternative to the either-or conceptualization. Learning can be thought of as a wheel and the particular characteristics of the analytical and global tendencies as spokes on the wheel. In this way, the various analytical and global learning skills summarized in Table 2.1 are attended to. The following questions can then be

Table 2.1. Analytical and Global Information Processing

Analytical Processing	Global Processing
Process information in a step-by-step manner	Process information in a simultaneous manner
Use logical inductive process	Use deductive or intuitive process
Perceive information in an abstract manner	Perceive information in a concrete manner
Perceive information in an objective manner	Perceive information in a subjective manner

asked: Where are the learners, teachers, text, or structures strong? Where can the teaching-learning exchange be improved?

As mentioned earlier, some adults are successful learners regardless of whether the teachers, text, or structures call for a more global or more analytical approach. Others are less successful because they have not "learned how to learn" (see Chapter Six for more on learning how to learn) in settings that differ from their own way of processing. Some analytical learners may not be successful in a global environment. For example, at a manufacturing firm, engineers are being taught how to be creative. They were initially so analytical in their thinking that when asked to brainstorm creative new products for the firm, they could only concentrate on the details of why their ideas would not be feasible. They had to be shown how to see the forest instead of the trees. On the other hand, some global learners are not successful in analytical settings. Often global learners have not been successful in school because schools tend to emphasize an analytical approach. These adult learners who find themselves in teaching-learning settings that perpetuate a school structure are likely to run into problems.

Opinions differ as to whether the settings should match learners' analytical or global processing styles, or whether they should challenge learners' processing styles by having the teaching, text, and structures support the opposite styles. I favor working in people's strongest processing mode until they have achieved some measure of learning success and perceived themselves as able to learn. Then they can be taught to learn how to learn in another processing mode. Figure 2.1 summarizes reasons why practitioners need an understanding of global and analytical processing.

Identifying Global and Analytical Characteristics

Global and analytical characteristics can be identified by using available instruments (see Chapter Five for criteria for instrument evaluation). Some instruments in particular focus on global and analytical information processing characteristics. The Hemispheric Mode Indicator, Herrmann's Brain Dominance Inventory, and Witkin's Group Embedded Figures Test are explained and their strengths and weaknesses discussed in Chapter Five. In addition to the instrument weaknesses mentioned in Chapter Five, other problems with using the instruments to determine global and analytical char-

Figure 2.1. Why Is Understanding Global and Analytical Processing Necessary?

To help learners overcome learning problems
To strengthen or introduce particular information processing characteristics
To enable learners to engage in holistic learning using both global and analytical
    learning strategies
To help learners learn how to learn

acteristics can be cited. First, in some of these instruments—for example, the Hemispheric Mode Indicator and Herrmann's Brain Dominance Inventory—people often answer in terms of how they perceive themselves to be rather than how they actually learn. Second, some instruments give one choice that is more global, one that is more analytical, and one that says the person learns well both ways. The idea is to find the holistic learners. However, what often happens is that many people select "both"—assuming that it is a more socially desirable answer—rather than selecting the one choice that reflects how they learn.

I suggest that practitioners do not need to use instruments but can identify global and analytical processing strategies in the instructional setting. Ask the learners to tell a story about the worst learning situation they ever experienced. Listen carefully to how they structure the story. Look for the global or analytical information processing characteristics (cited in Table 2.1) of how they tell the story.

You can also review the teaching plans, texts, or setting to determine which cognitive style is being stressed in the learning setting. Whether considering the teaching, texts, or structures, use the information in Figure 2.2 as a guide to critique the global and analytical aspects present and then to adapt the plan, text, or structures for the future.

Teaching Global and Analytical Learners

Teaching, texts, and structures can be adapted to teach global or analytical information processors. From what has been said thus far, think of the global and analytical emphases in your teaching now. List them on a slip of paper and label them global or analytical. Note which specific aspect of the global or analytical approach you are addressing.

I also offer the following suggestions:

• To develop global skills of brainstorming, have learners guess the answers to the question they want to ask. Create as many project ideas as possible. No idea is bad or impossible. The only responses allowed from other learners are "yes, if . . ." For example, in a planning session on how to disseminate information on AIDS, someone may suggest dropping leaflets from

Figure 2.2. Global and Analytical Review Guide for Teaching
Plans, Texts, and Structures

1. Look at your teaching plan, the text plan, or the classroom or school structures.
2. Mark each step or aspect of the plan, text, or structure as global or analytical.
3. Consider learners' difficulties.
4. Consider your goals regarding use of global and analytical processing, as noted in Figure 2.1.
5. Decide which global or analytical skill you want to stress.
6. Adjust your plan, text, or structure accordingly.

a plane. Those hearing the suggestion must respond to the idea, "yes, if . . ." "Yes, if it can get people's attention."

• To develop the analytical skills of picking out discrete parts from content, provide an outline of the most important items in the order in which you will treat them. This will assist the more global learners, who have difficulty in distinguishing important points, since it will give them an external structure for the presentation.

• Vary outline structures of information to be learned. For analytical learners, the preferred structure is linear and sequential, as shown on the left side of Figure 2.3. For global learners, the preferred structure is global and simultaneous, as shown on the right side of Figure 2.3.

• The outlines provided for the learners should have lots of white space for the global learners, who, as note takers, write down as much information as possible. Global learners also tend to sequence the information exactly as it is presented (Frank, 1984). Global learners can be misled by irrelevant information or by interference in the train of thought on the part of the instructor.

• For note taking, provide a hierarchical outline and teach from it. This gives global learners the external structures they need to encode the information and to be able to distinguish important points. Analytical learners sample fully from the given materials and will usually reject irrelevant information, but because they use less salient cues in developing hypotheses, proofs, and arguments, they can at times attain the wrong concept.

• Develop global processing skills by encouraging the development of outlines such as the global one in Figure 2.3. Sometimes called *mind maps,* these nonlinear structures help learners jot down ideas they have read or want to write about, then group them in ways that make sense to them. Works by Buzan (1980) and Williams (1982) detail more about mind mapping.

• For analytical learners, begin each teaching-learning exchange with a short outline of what will be presented, then present the material. For global learners, begin each teaching-learning exchange with a sense of what is to

Figure 2.3. Global and Analytical Structuring of Information

Global Outline

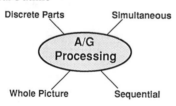

Analytical Outline

I. Ways of processing information
   A. Analytical
      1. Discrete parts
      2. Sequential
   B. Global
      1. Whole picture
      2. Simultaneous

come. Follow this by making a connection to what is concrete and important to them. You could tell a brief story in which the points to be made are embedded; at the end, either you or the learners should give the important points of the story.

For example, if you are trying to teach certain management principles, historical facts, or grammar or math rules, begin with the abstract principles or rules, for the analytical learners. Then proceed to look at the definitions of these and how to use them. Deal at the end with their use in the work or learning setting. Analytical learners tend to learn more rapidly from abstract cues and tend to learn more incidental subject material at the expense of social cues. For global learners, a problem they have experienced in a work setting or a case study of a learning setting would be the opener. Aspects of what was going on would be discussed, followed by trying to determine the rules that might govern the situation. Remember that global learners tend to learn better (more rapidly) when given relevant and concrete examples. Because global learners perceive less distinction between self and nonself, they tend to learn more from incident-social material than from incident-subject material.

• Because global learners attend to the whole picture, they often have difficulty with the precision demanded by math. Encourage global learners to use rounding of numbers to get a sense of where their answer should fall. Insist that global learners trace heavily with a pencil or marker over the mathematical signs of a problem before beginning to solve it, so that they attend to the correct procedure. At the end, they should check to make sure that they have in fact carried out the proper operations.

• Because of their interest in the larger picture, global learners are also unlikely to attend to details like punctuation. These are irrelevant to the story. Teach punctuation to global learners by attaching it to the pauses that occur naturally when the actual story is told, rather than by teaching punctuation rules, which global learners perceive as abstract.

• In language learning, global learners acquire a dialect more effectively through interaction with speakers of that dialect (the concrete and subjective) than through being constantly corrected. They learn to write not by being taught grammatical and other skills, but by writing in meaningful contexts.

• Analytical learners are more likely to attend to math signs and punctuation with diligence. Work to have analytical learners estimate math results and put the punctuation on hold and concentrate on truly creative writing.

• Use of graphics and visual aids follows much of what has been said above. Here are some specific pointers:

Help global learners by simplifying graphic materials. This will decrease the level of abstraction and will help these learners distinguish the important parts from the whole.

Provide a well-structured explanation of what the learner should attend to in a graphic or visual aid. Without external direction, global learners may have to spend the same amount of time and effort in disembedding the material to be learned from a complex picture as they would spend in reading a detailed description.

Present the graphic or visual aid when the information is presented.

Keep it in front of the learners the entire time during which reference to that material is being made.

If multiple graphics are to be used and if they are closely related to one another, all of the graphics should be displayed during that part of the presentation. This aids the global learner in accepting the information in the sequence presented and in processing it as part of the immediate field of perception. Showing the graphic later or removing it from view during the discussion tends to separate the information provided by the graphic from the information being discussed.

• Global and analytical learners encode memories differently. (See Chapter Four for more information on how memory works.) Analytical learners tend to sort and encode information as it is being received because as they learn, they presort and organize. Global learners, because they take in the whole picture at once, have less short-term memory capacity. There is too much material taken in, in no apparent order. Global learners need to have structured support in going back to the material, organizing it, and relating it to what is important to them and to what they have previously learned. Active tasks designed to help with understanding, storage, and recall should be used. Learners can use colored pens to underline what is important, draw pictures they think of next to important notes, place clusters of associated facts in various corners of their papers, and use mind mapping to connect pieces.

• Assessment usually demands analytical processing. As was suggested in Chapter One, evaluation needs to reflect the processing being attended to. If global and analytical learners are to be supported in their efforts to learn, evaluation must also be designed that demands global processing. Use essay questions instead of multiple-choice or true-false alternatives. Or, instead of using basic true-false items, have the learners explain why the answer is true or false. Have them tell a story or construct a case study that embodies the principles being emphasized and assessed.

• Global and analytical information processing are not related to any particular perceptual modality styles (see Chapter One). That is, global learners or analytical learners will not show preference for one modality or another (Manfredo, 1987). What is important is that global learners will extract different information than analytical learners from the same stimulus, whether the stimulus is visual, haptic, aural, or another type. People who tend to use an analytical processing style in one modality tend to use the same analytical style in other modalities (Goodenough, 1976). As Eric and Felicia participate in the same training session, they may or may not have the same perceptual modalities, but because their global and analytical cognitive information processing characteristics are different, their responses to the verbal and visual material will be different. Eric will abstract the gist of what is presented; Felicia will take in the details of the material covered.

Conclusion

Information processing varies for different individuals. This chapter has attended to the two aspects of cognitive information processing called global and analytical. Global processing involves the ability to take in information as a whole, simultaneously, deductively, concretely, and subjectively. Analytical processing involves the ability to take in information in discrete parts, sequentially, logically, abstractly, and objectively. People differ in their ability to process information globally and analytically. Learning settings, including teachers, texts, and school or class structures, promote global and analytical information processing to different degrees. A match does not always exist between the information processing promoted by the learning settings and the strengths of the learners. For some learners, this incongruity results in a lack of success in the teaching-learning exchange. In attending to global and analytical information processing, educators must do four things. First, they must decide what they believe the information processing strengths of the learners should be with regard to global and analytical information processing. Second, they must check which processing skills the learners possess. Third, they must either find ways to teach the needed global and analytical skills to the learners or else match their teaching, texts, and structures to the learners' information processing strengths. Finally, teachers must deliberately and frequently critique their teaching plans with regard to the particular skills within global and analytical processing they are utilizing in their teaching to see if indeed their practice reflects these information processing skills.

References

Buzan, T. *Using Both Sides of Your Brain.* New York: Dutton, 1980.

Cawley, R. W., Miller, S. A., and Milligan, J. N. "Cognitive Styles and the Adult Learner." *Adult Education,* 1976, 27 (2), 101–116.

Cohen, R. A. "Conceptual Styles, Culture, Conflict, and Nonverbal Tests of Intelligence." *American Anthropologist,* 1969, 71, 828–856.

Cranston, M., and McCort, B. "A Learner Analysis Experiment: Cognitive Style vs. Learning Style in Undergraduate Nursing Education." *Journal of Nursing Education,* 1985, 24, 136–138.

Flannery, D. D. "The Relationship of Analytical and Global Learning Strategies to Persistence in Writing a Dissertation." *Proceedings for the Project for the Study of Adult Learning.* Bloomington: College of Continuing Education and Public Service, Illinois State University, 1991.

Frank, B. M. "Effect of Field Independence-Dependence and Study Technique on Learning from a Lecture." *American Education Research Journal,* 1984, 21, 669–678.

Goodenough, D. R. "The Role of Individual Differences in Field Dependence as a Factor in Learn-
ing and Memory." *Psychological Bulletin,* 1976, *83,* 675–694.
Herrmann, N. *The Creative Brain.* Lake Luree, N.C.: Brain Books, 1990.
Levy, J. "Psychological Implications of Bilateral Asymmetry." In S. Diamond and G. Beaumont
(eds.), *Hemispheric Function in the Human Brain.* New York: Halsted Press, 1974.
Luria, A. R. *The Working Brain: An Introduction to Neuropsychology.* New York: Basic Books, 1973.
Manfredo, P. A. "Dimensions of Cognitive Style: Their Interrelationships and Use in Maximizing
Trainability." Unpublished master's thesis, Louisiana State University, 1987. (ED 307 522)
Ornstein, R. E. *The Psychology of Consciousness.* New York: Viking, 1972.
Schmeck, R. R. *Learning Strategies and Learning Styles.* New York: Plenum, 1988.
Smith, R. M. *Learning How to Learn: Applied Theory for Adults.* New York: Cambridge University
Press, 1982.
Williams, L. V. *Teaching for the Two-Sided Mind.* Englewood Cliffs, N.J.: Prentice Hall, 1982.
Witkin, H. A., Moore, C. A., Goodenough, D. R., and Cox, P. W. "Field-Dependent and Field-
Independent Cognitive Styles and Their Educational Implications." *Review of Educational
Research,* 1977, *47,* 1–64.

*DANIELE D. FLANNERY is assistant professor of adult education and coordinator of
the adult education Doctor of Education program at The Pennsylvania State University, Harrisburg.*

Learning is not just the acquisition and manipulation of content; how and how well we learn is influenced by the affective realm—our emotions and feelings—as well as by the cognitive domain.

The Influence of Affective Processing in Education and Training

Trenton R. Ferro

The concept of education that both educators of adults and adult students bring to the learning situation has been shaped by the experience of schooling. That experience has been one where education was primarily a process of learning (often isolated and unrelated) facts that were then repeated, hopefully to the satisfaction of teachers who exercised sole control and authority in the classroom—an experience described as "fill and drill." To learn these facts properly and demonstrate mastery of them, learners sat quietly in rows and completed worksheets and other repetitive exercises. Such educational activities and environments were devoid of any concept of the value of experience or the expression of emotion and feelings. Recognized as an integral part of so many other aspects of life, the affective domain had no place in the teaching-learning exchange. In fact, superintendents, principals, and even parents considered any activity other than the cognitive as detrimental to the learning process. Rather than viewing teachers who utilized emotive and affective practices as innovative, observers often judged these teachers to be incompetent and incapable of maintaining order and discipline in their classrooms.

Experience tells us that this model of the educational process was, and is, inadequate. Many performed poorly according to these standards; some inherited the label of "troublemaker"; others passed through the system satisfactorily, in spite of personal discomfort and dissatisfaction with the learning environment. In each case, the setting did not fit well with how learners might best learn. Recent advances in brain research, as noted in this chapter, help to explain why most of us are not at our best in learning situations devoid of affective elements. While Chapters One and Two have focused on cognitive aspects of learning, this chapter highlights the role of the affective realm—the emotions and the feelings—in the process of learning.

Understanding the Triune Brain

The human brain is the culmination of a long, sequential, and hierarchical developmental process (MacLean, 1978). Three formations of the brain have evolved, each developing as the means to cope with various threats and circumstances in the world. Each of the three brains, which together form the *triune brain,* controls and guides certain aspects of people's total complex of behaviors.

The earliest brain, the reptilian brain (R-complex), controls actions related to physical activity, safety, and the maintenance of the body. Bodily functions, such as digestion and breathing; ritualistic behaviors related to courtship and mating as well as territoriality; and the fight-or-flight responses to stress are all governed by the R-complex. The various functions controlled by the R-complex are instinctive.

The next brain, the paleomammalian brain (limbic system), is involved primarily with the experience and expression of emotion. Only those creatures with a limbic brain are devoted to the care and raising of their young. Emotions related to memories (as illustrated by such experiences as déjà vu) are also the province of the limbic system. We will return shortly to this remarkable brain.

The latest brain, the neomammalian brain (neocortex), is the cognitive, or thinking, brain and the brain that was the basis for the discussions in Chapters One and Two. The neocortex receives, codes, and stores the various messages transmitted to the brain from the senses; it is also the center of creativity, problem solving, abstraction, and the use of symbols that allows mathematical and verbal communication (MacLean, 1978; Sagan, 1977).

Although actions or behaviors, emotions or feelings, and concepts or abstractions of the three brains can be distinguished analytically, all three brain formations are connected in the triune brain. For example, the limbic system is active during every function of the R-complex and the neocortex. When new information enters the brain through the senses, both the facts and the feelings are stored in memory (Ornstein and Thompson, 1984). The limbic system also determines the response to information received. Since each experience includes an emotional dimension, an emotional reaction is part of each person's response to a situation. The memories triggered by any new experience include the memory of the feelings and emotions that accompanied the original experience. If the original experience was one of happiness, delight, joy, or pleasure, the response to a current situation that has triggered that memory will be similar. If, on the other hand, the original experience caused anxiety or fear and triggered a fight-or-flight response, the reaction to the current situation will also be anxiety or fear. The limbic system will signal the R-complex to avoid the new situation in a manner similar to the response utilized at the time of the former experience, now recalled from memory. This is called *downshifting* (Hart, 1983; Caine and Caine, 1991). Control of the person's thoughts and actions has shifted "down" from the neocortex to the R-complex. When such downshifting occurs, the individual becomes obsessed with self-preservation; the neocortex, or thinking brain, is placed, in effect, on hold.

An example of this was related by participants in the New York State Adult Life Management Program. These adults indicated that by the time they had reached the second grade, most of them had both experienced failure and accepted as their personal story the belief that they were, in fact, failures (Ferro, 1992). These beliefs were lived out with both passive and aggressive patterns of behavior designed to cover the inner sense of shame and low self-esteem. These behavior patterns were intended to foster self-preservation. Before any attitudinal change could take place, these stories with their attendant emotional baggage had to be identified and shared; only then could the limbic system redirect the emotional message to the neocortex so that growth and learning could occur.

The focus of this chapter is on the affective domain in learning. Yet, as noted above, the affective (limbic system) cannot be conceptualized apart from other parts of the brain when attending to learning. We will deal first with affect (the limbic system) itself, then consider the interrelatedness of the limbic system with the R-complex and the neocortex in the teaching-learning exchange.

Attention to the Affective Domain in Adult Education

The important role of the affective domain has been discussed in adult education literature and practice. It has been acknowledged that learners bring feelings of self-esteem, fear, respect for authority, need for status, comfort with varying amounts of autonomy or structure, and previous experience in schools to their learning transactions (Kidd, 1973; Smith, 1982). However, "while these factors are recognized by some, learning is often looked upon and spoken of as if it were entirely an intellectual exercise" (Kidd, 1973, p. 94).

In an effort to include the affective component, researchers and practitioners offer a range of affective strategies for the teaching-learning exchange itself, for curriculum development, for supporting returning adult students, and for teaching learning how to learn for the affective level.

To incorporate affect into the teaching-learning exchange, the following measures are important:

Recognize the value of previous experience, emphasize the necessity of upholding the self-esteem of adult learners, and stress the importance of attending to environmental factors in the learning setting (Smith, 1982; Kidd, 1973).

Provide for security and for both dependence and independence in the learning transaction. Build on relationships. Stimulate learners to engage in learning, and facilitate satisfaction and achievement for them (Kidd, 1973).

"Selectively emphasize and deal with the human perspective of what is being learned, with application to the personal daily lives of the adult learners whenever possible" (Wlodkowski, 1985, p. 190).

"Relate content and instructional procedures to learner concerns" (Wlodkowski, 1985, p. 192).

"Selectively relate content and instructional procedures to learner values. "[Do] . . . not . . . be dogmatic or . . . moralize about value-laden topics unless there is an exceptionally good reason to do so. . . . Introduce the topic as one that reflects differing values and . . . serve as a moderator with no particular advocacy. Present a concept or a skill at the value level of learning, with personal acceptance and application at the prerogative of the individual learner. . . . Encourage an atmosphere of mutual respect and allow each adult personal choice in matters of opinion, selection, and application" (Wlodkowski, 1985, pp. 192–194).

"Deal with and encourage the expression of emotions during learning" (Wlodkowski, 1985, p. 194).

"Help learners to directly experience cognitive concepts on a physical and emotional level" (Wlodkowski, 1985, p. 195).

Incorporating the affective dimension in the entire process of *curriculum development* has been the goal of the New York State Adult Life Management Program. The "Dance of Learning" is a nine-step instructional delivery system utilized in the planning of the program's modules and lessons (Dyer, 1987; Ferro, 1992). The steps of the delivery system are summarized as follows:

1. Create the spark: Plan activities that pique the learner's interest in preparation for what is to come.
2. Step into partnership: Invite students to join teachers in the dance by telling them what they have been doing and allowing them to say what they would like to learn.
3. Share experiences: Encourage learners to share their stories, allowing teachers to learn how, when, and why students have problems learning and why they learn as they do.
4. Decode what is new: Show the big picture, then the pieces; ground the new in the known.
5. Bridge the gap: Involve the whole person—mind, body, and spirit—by using sensory learning strategies to tie the new information in with what is already known.

6. Try it out: Move from telling and showing to doing.
7. Feedback: Allow the learners the opportunity to reflect on their new experience and to develop their own internal story.
8. Step up to life: Via planned activities, transfer the learning to real-life situations.
9. Step out: Make the learning a natural part of each learner's daily life.

Daloz (1986), concerned with the emotional level and difficult transitions of *returning adult students*, suggests a supportive mentoring relationship between student and facilitator. This relationship should encourage adult students to get in touch with the emotional level of the transitions they face. First, mentors must support the participants by "affirming the validity of the students' present experience" (p. 212), listening, providing structure, expressing positive expectations, serving as advocates, sharing themselves, and making the relationship special (pp. 215–223). Second, mentors must challenge the students to face the emotions inherent in returning to school "by setting tasks, engaging in discussion, 'heating up dichotomies' (increasing pressure for resolution by taking differing or opposite perspectives), constructing hypotheses, and setting high standards" (pp. 223–229). Third, mentors must provide vision. "They must help the students to look ahead, to form their own dreams, to sketch their own maps" (p. 214) by modeling, keeping tradition, offering a map, suggesting new language, and providing a mirror (pp. 229–234).

Finally, learners must be taught to *learn how to learn* (for more, see Chapter Six) affectively. Gibbons (1990, pp. 84–85) outlines three goals in this learning-how-to-learn process: "The first goal is learning how to identify and eliminate those inner states that are inhibitory to learning, such as emotional numbness or artificiality, personal confusion, insecurity, helplessness, and self-doubt. The second is learning how to establish those inner states that are enabling, such as authentic feeling, clarity, confidence, determination, and trust in our own judgment. The third is learning how to access or build the intensity of caring, pleasure, and power that are involved in passionate pursuit."

Interrelatedness of the Three Brains

Emotion cannot be separated from learning. Various approaches to considering the interrelationships among the dimensions of the triune brain in the learning process have been suggested. Two models will be discussed here: the taxonomy of educational objectives and the Pierce-Gray classification model.

The taxonomy of educational objectives (Bloom and others, 1956; Harrow, 1972; Krathwohl, Bloom, and Masia, 1964) is a classification system intended to provide a "large over-all scheme or matrix" (Krathwohl, Bloom, and Masia, 1964, p. 4). The desired end was a holistic model that would encompass the full range of possible educational goals and outcomes. In so doing, the classification system would delineate the specific skills of the affective, cognitive, and psychomotor domains and demonstrate the connectedness among the domains.

For purposes of this chapter on affective processing, it should be noted that the specific skills of the affective domain as conceptualized by Krathwohl, Bloom, and Masia (1964) include receiving or attending to stimuli, responding by committing oneself to being involved, valuing particular behavior, organizing one's values into a system of relationships, and developing an internally consistent system of values. Originally in the use of the taxonomy of educational objectives, as much emphasis in statements of objectives was given to affective objectives as to cognitive objectives. However, over time, affective objectives were dropped from statements about courses, and efforts at appraisal of student growth in the affective domain almost disappeared (Krathwohl, Bloom, and Masia, 1964). This erosion was abetted by a "hesitation in the use of affective measures for grading purposes" due, in large part, "to philosophical and cultural values" that hold that "one's beliefs, attitudes, values, and personality characteristics are more likely to be regarded as private matters, except in the most extreme instances" (Krathwohl, Bloom, and Masia, 1964, pp. 17–18). Furthermore, there is still an implicit belief that if cognitive objectives are developed and attended to, a corresponding development of appropriate affective behaviors will occur. Research does not support this thesis.

The Pierce-Gray classification model (Table 3.1) is based on Pierce and Gray's (1981) analysis of fourteen different classification systems, which they integrated into their own system. Assumptions for this model are similar to those of the taxonomy of educational objectives. This model emphasizes (1) the parallels that exist between the domains and (2) the integration that occurs among the domains, especially at the higher levels. Each of the three domains is constantly interacting with the other two. The cognitive domain is influenced by, and is influencing, both the affective and psychomotor domains. In turn, the affective and psychomotor domains are influencing each other. The Pierce-Gray model places less emphasis on values and valuing in the affective domain than the taxonomy of educational objectives does.

Table 3.1. Pierce-Gray Classification Model

Cognitive Domain	Affective Domain	Psychomotor Domain
Cognitive creating	Affective creating	Psychomotor creating
Cognitive judging	Affective judging	Psychomotor judging
Analyzing	Validating	Maneuvering
Applying	Conforming	Executing
Understanding	Reacting	Activating
Cognitive perceiving	Affective perceiving	Psychomotor perceiving

Rather, Pierce and Gray characterize the affective domain as a sensing that things are okay, as feeling what is right, and as being emotionally creative.

The importance of these models for our purposes is that the instructional process must attend to all three domains of educational objectives, not just to the cognitive, as often happens. Not only is developing and teaching to objectives at all levels in all three domains important, but it is necessary, because this is how people really think, learn, grow, feel, and act. Only then is the whole person involved.

Relationship to Instructional Design

The preceding discussion has made a case for including affective elements in every training session, workshop, program, course, or seminar. Further, the discussion has stressed the interrelationships among the cognitive, affective, and psychomotor realms in the teaching-learning exchange. Desired outcomes in most learning situations include the following: expanded knowledge, appropriate attitudes, and improved action patterns. For example, a Pennsylvania Department of Education Act 353 project called "Musically Speaking" shows "music inspires emotions. One of the premises is that emotions can help the English as a second language student to internalize the vocabulary, grammatical strutures [sic], and idioms they are studying" (Mace, 1993, p. 4).

In a second example, the New York State Adult Life Management Program (Dyer, 1987; Ferro, 1992) has demonstrated that emotion is tied to motion; the use of kinesthetic strategies affects the affective domain. One such activity involves a "koosh" ball: With the group in a circle, the ball is tossed from member to member. Only the person holding the ball may speak; other members may not interrupt. This activity has helped people with low self-esteem gain a feeling of self-worth. Few desired learning outcomes do not require attention to all three domains.

"Recent brain research indicates the necessity of emotional engagement during learning to maintain motivation for learning" (Wlodkowski, 1985, p. 178). Of related importance is the learning environment. The literature on adults as learners is filled with advice regarding attention to such matters as heat, light, room arrangement, and the location of classes at sites that do not trigger memories of previous negative experiences. Careful attention to the affective domain can increase learner motivation and counteract, or at least minimize, the affects of such memories. Recognizing the connection between memory and emotion helps us understand what happens to many adults when they reenter a classroom for the first time after they have left formal schooling. Emotion-laden memories flood back. If earlier experiences were negative or ambivalent, those same feelings are present. As mentioned above, adults' personal stories—thoughts that they are stupid or ignorant and that they cannot learn—now programmed into their beings, may arrive in the classroom with them. Before facilitators can proceed, they must deal with the emotional baggage prospective participants carry into the classroom. The tendency of many adults to downshift because of past experience should give administrators, supervisors, and planners pause when they consider where to conduct their programs. Moving away from sites such as traditional school settings that trigger such negative responses and that may interfere with cognitive learning, could be the first step in applying affective learning theory.

Another implication of understanding the role of the limbic system within the conceptual framework of the brain is knowing what happens when people are under stress. We know that there is both *eustress* and *distress* (Selye, 1978). More recent research has shown that the body produces one type of hormone when a stressful situation is seen as a challenge (eustress) and a different type of hormone when the stressful situation is seen as a threat (distress) to a person's capability to function and the stressor appears inescapable (Dienstbier, 1989). Thus, the emotional response of the individual to a specific situation plays a determining role in that person's cognitive functioning—either to fight, resist, or avoid the learning situation or to be open to new opportunities. "The underlying message is that mental and emotional responses affect the functioning and operating of the body. Body and mind, therefore, influence each other" (Caine and Caine, 1991, p. 65). Educators of adults will want to examine the atmosphere of their learning settings; the types, manner, and methods of testing procedures; and the various methods, strategies, and techniques they use. Do these experiences foster eustress or distress? Is the learning setting challenging the learners to greater involvement and participation, or is it causing them to downshift into a fight-or-flight mode, thereby effectively blocking the active functioning of the neocortex, the thinking brain?

Recognizing the tremendous impact the affective domain has on how adults function and learn will lead facilitators to seek out strategies that both tap into the affective realm and effectively use it to enhance the overall cognitive process.

Conclusion

These strategies work because they deal with the affective elements—emotions and feelings. By establishing high trust levels, fostering an accepting atmosphere, and creating positive self-awareness and self-concept, they encourage participants to become involved in group activities and the learning process. In terms of brain function, the limbic system interprets these strategies as desirable. Its messages involve the neocortex and create eustress with the attendant hormones, which cause the individual to rise to the challenge. Since the emotions are involved in every learning transaction, trainers and facilitators must attend to the affective domain. They do this by setting affective objectives as well as cognitive ones, by creating a comfortable atmosphere, by selecting the appropriate activities, and by attending to learners' emotional responses.

References

Bloom, B., Englehart, M. D., Furst, E. J., Hill, W. H., and Krathwohl, D. R. *Taxonomy of Educational Objectives: The Classification of Educational Goals.* Handbook 1: *Cognitive Domain.* New York: McKay, 1956.

Caine, R. N., and Caine, G. *Making Connections: Teaching and the Human Brain.* Alexandria, Va.: Association for Supervision and Curriculum Development, 1991.

Daloz, L. A. *Effective Teaching and Mentoring: Realizing the Transformational Power of Adult Learning Experiences.* San Francisco: Jossey-Bass, 1986.

Dienstbier, R. A. "Arousal and Physiological Toughness: Implications for Mental and Physical Health." *Psychological Review,* 1989, *96* (1), 84–100.

Dyer, A. F. "Development of Model Guidelines for Implementing a Classroom Management System in Life Skills Education in New York State." Unpublished doctoral dissertation, Nova University, 1987.

Ferro, T. R. *Final Report, Research and Evaluation Project: New York State Adult Life Management Program.* Albany: Two Year College Development Center, State University of New York at Albany, 1992.

Gibbons, M. "A Working Model of the Learning-How-to-Learn Process." In R. M. Smith and Associates, *Learning to Learn Across the Life Span.* San Francisco: Jossey-Bass, 1990.

Harrow, A. J. *A Taxonomy of the Psychomotor Domain.* New York: McKay, 1972.

Hart, L. *Human Brain, Human Learning.* White Plains, N.Y.: Longman, 1983.

Kidd, J. R. *How Adults Learn.* (Rev. ed.) New York: Cambridge University Press, 1973.

Krathwohl, D. R., Bloom, B. S., and Masia, B. B. *Taxonomy of Educational Objectives: The Classification of Educational Goals.* Handbook 11: *Affective Domain.* White Plains, N.Y.: Longman, 1964.

Mace, D. "Musically Speaking." *What's the Buzz?* May 1993, p. 4.

MacLean, P. D. "A Mind of Three Minds: Educating the Triune Brain." In J. S. Chall and A. F. Mirsky (eds.), *Education and the Brain.* The 77th yearbook of the National Society for the Study of Education. Chicago: National Society for the Study of Education, 1978.

Ornstein, R. E., and Thompson, R. F. *The Amazing Brain.* Boston: Houghton Mifflin, 1984.

Pierce, W. D., and Gray, C. E. *Deciphering the Learning Domains: A Second Generation Classification Model for Education Objectives.* Washington, D.C.: University Presses of America, 1981.

Sagan, C. *The Dragons of Eden: Speculations on the Evolution of Human Intelligence.* New York: Ballantine, 1977.

Selye, H. *The Stress of Life.* (Rev. ed.) New York: McGraw-Hill, 1978.

Smith, R. M. *Learning How to Learn: Applied Theory for Adults.* New York: Cambridge University Press, 1982.

Wlodkowski, R. J. *Enhancing Adult Motivation to Learn: A Guide to Improving Instruction and Increasing Learner Achievement.* San Francisco: Jossey-Bass, 1985.

TRENTON R. FERRO *is assistant professor of adult and community education and coordinator of the Master of Arts program in adult and community education at Indiana University of Pennsylvania.*

The structural model of human memory and its major processing
operations are linked with their application to teaching and learning.

Memory Is Not Only About Storage

Kay L. Huber

Human memory and learning are inextricably linked. Without learning, there is nothing to remember, and without memory, there is no evidence of learning (Baddeley, 1989; Long, 1983; Schaie and Geiwitz, 1982). A significant amount of human learning is unintentional and occurs unconsciously through everyday exposure to a wide array of stimuli. This chapter focuses on intentional learning processes that occur when we take in and interpret information. Memory is the mechanism by which that information is stored and retrieved. Memory, a more abstract process than learning, is conceptualized in a variety of ways.

Memory Structures and Processes

In 1968, Atkinson and Shiffrin proposed a dual-store model of memory that had three components: sensory memory, short-term memory, and long-term memory. Each component had a different capacity for the length of time information was stored. Since then, this structural model—or slight variations of it—has been the predominant view of human memory (Botwinick, 1984; Craik, 1977; Merriam and Caffarella, 1991; Ormrod, 1990; Poon, 1985; Salthouse, 1991; Schaie and Willis, 1986).

Sensory memory, lasting less than one second, consists of completely unorganized material that is registered via auditory, visual, or tactile senses. Auditory, or echoic, memory lasts several seconds and is critical for understanding speech. Visual, or iconic, memory generally lasts less than one second unless an individual has a photographic memory (Leahey and Harris, 1989).

The most active processing of information occurs in *short-term,* or *work-*

ing, memory, where material can be retained from five to thirty seconds. The material in short-term memory includes everything being thought about at the moment (Leahey and Harris, 1989). Working memory has a very small storage capacity, and unless processing of information continues, the information is lost.

Long-term memory appears to have limitless capacity and storage that lasts for years or decades. Information stored in long-term memory may be episodic, autobiographical material that is a record of events connected with time and place (learning an item-number relationship on a specific occasion), or semantic, organized knowledge about words, symbols, their meanings, relationships, and the rules for manipulating them (learning a permanent fact such as the alphabet, then putting it together into words and using the words to form correct sentences) (Bootzin, Loftus, and Zajonc, 1983). Information is most likely to be stored in long-term memory when it is organized and integrated with information already stored there (Ormrod, 1990).

A variety of mental activities have been conceived to account for the way information is processed in memory. The most common model divides the major processing operations into three phases (Poon, 1985; Salthouse, 1991; Schaie and Willis, 1986). The first, *encoding,* or acquisition, is a way of putting information into appropriate form for later use. Encoding involves multiple processes ranging from analysis of sensory stimuli to extensive elaboration and organization of information in conjunction with existing knowledge (Salthouse, 1991). The second phase, *storage,* or retention, entails filing or preserving information. The third phase, *retrieval,* involves processes such as recognition and recall that are used to make stored information accessible for use. Potter (1990) points out that memories decay over time. Stronger memories have a greater probability of being retrieved more often and with more speed. As time passes, memory strength is reduced. Recalling or recognizing something increases its memory strength and slows the rate of forgetting. Storage and retrieval occur in all three components of the common memory model, while encoding occurs in only short- and long-term memory.

Mental operations also vary with respect to attentional requirements. *Attention,* or attending to, appears to be essential in moving information from sensory to short-term memory. The process of attention is used for both information selection and determination of the amount of attention required for processing operations. Automatic processes can be executed with little or no demands on attention, whereas effortful processes can only operate when they are supplied with, or monitored by, attention (Salthouse, 1991). For example, people can carry on a conversation while driving a car unless demanding conditions exist that require full attention to the activity of driving. Effortful, or controlled, processes must generally be executed serially because they require so much attention, while automatic processes may be executed in parallel (Leahey and Harris, 1989).

The aging process has almost always been accompanied by a perceived decline in the ability to acquire and remember information. As Poon (1985, pp. 427) states, "The feeling that one's ability to remember and to retrieve information is not as good as it used to be is a universal complaint among middle-aged and elderly persons." Research on memory and memory and aging has examined both memory function and the perceived effect of aging on memory processes.

Memory Research

Memory research has been dominated by experimental, laboratory-based traditions for most of the past century. This research approach began in 1879 when Ebbinghaus used himself as the subject of the first experimental investigation of learning and memory (Gregg, 1986; Hoffman, Bringman, Bamberg, and Klein, 1987). Around the same time, Sir Francis Galton was considering the richness and complexity of memory in the real world; however, his contribution to memory research was largely neglected for nearly eighty years (Baddeley, 1989). Therefore, current knowledge about memory functions has come primarily from laboratory-based research with cross-sectional designs. This research was largely limited to the retention of content that was under the direct control of an experimenter, that was presented during a few hours or less, that was emotionally and motivationally neutral, and that was tested for retention within a short time following acquisition (Bahrick, 1989). The study of memory and its relationship to aging has focused on comparing the performance of young and old adults on the same tasks. This methodology calls into question whether or not the outcomes reflected age and cohort differences or age changes.

Growing numbers of researchers are studying memory in the context of everyday adult lives. Landauer (1989, p. 118) points out that "if the mind is studied only in the laboratory, it will be very easy to miss some of the functions for which it is designed, some of the environmental and experiential support on which its function depends, and some of the obstacles with which it needs to contend." This research fosters what is known as *ecological validity*, meaning that it is assumed that the tasks being studied are personally meaningful and reflect the experiences of adults in their natural environment.

The outcomes of laboratory-based research point to age-related deficits, primarily in long-term memory in the areas of encoding, storage, and retrieval of material and in the level and speed of processing information (Craik, 1977; Hayslip and Panek, 1989; Rybash, Hoyer, and Roodin, 1986; Salthouse, 1982; Schaie and Willis, 1986). This general-decrement principle is being challenged by researchers interested in the contextual conceptualization of memory where fewer age-related declines have been found. Memory researchers need to develop ways to assess everyday memory performance in laboratory settings without sacrificing external validity. Until then, it remains an open question whether the declines demonstrated in the laboratory manifest themselves in the classroom and in the everyday functions and learning activities of adults (Lavigne and Finley, 1990; Merriam and Caffarella, 1991; Peterson, 1983).

Application of Memory Processes to Teaching and Learning

It is important to remember the link between learning and memory before considering the application of memory processes to teaching-learning situations. Intentional learning processes and memory processes (acquisition, storage, and retrieval) are probably synonymous terms because the same factors that affect learning also affect memory. Processing information is influenced by whether the learner experiences the environment in a global or an analytical cognitive style. The perceptual modality preference of the learner also influences information processing. Noncognitive factors (such as fear of failure, anxiety, depression, and certain medications) affect learning and memory performance. The most successful and effective application of memory processes should occur in a supportive educational environment and should be preceded by an analysis of the learner's cognitive style.

Ormrod (1990) believes that four general principles of memory have particular relevance for education: (1) attention, the process by which information moves from sensory memory into short-term memory, is essential for learning; (2) short-term memory is the bottleneck in the human memory system because of its limited capacity and the short length of time information remains there; (3) memory is selective because learners must continually make choices about what information to focus on and what information to ignore; and (4) the limited capacity of short-term memory forces learners to condense, organize, and synthesize the information they receive.

Keeping these principles in mind, the processing operations of cognition and memory will be discussed by organizing them under the three major components of the structural model of memory: sensory, short-term, and long-term memory. It is important to note that some of these processes will appear more than once and that many of them are interdependent.

Sensory Memory. Visual memory supports initial perception and auditory memory supports language comprehension. In the initial second or two after new visual or auditory information arrives, it is actively processed by being attended to, recognized, interpreted, and if selected, moved into short-term memory to be related to other information (Potter, 1990). Auditory memory lasts longer than visual memory; therefore, combining these two perceptual modalities enhances instruction. Peterson (1983) points out that several studies support improvement in learning when the learner is provided visual images while simultaneously hearing the material. Increased learning is likely to result if the instructor uses transparencies, the chalkboard, or written outlines to list important points.

Attention is the early process by which we select information for cognitive processing (Lapp, 1987; Leahey and Harris, 1989; Ormrod, 1990; Salthouse, 1991). Attention may be the state of concentrating on something or it may be seen as a processing capacity that can be parceled out to different stimuli and activities. There are a variety of factors—such as size, intensity, emotion, and personal significance—that influence attention. Instructors may use print material with letters of various sizes, bright colors, or emotionally strong stimuli to attract the attention of the learner.

Selection—choosing information to process—means that individuals must have a means of determining what is important and what is not. Determination of the importance of new information depends, in part, on knowledge already stored in long-term memory. For instance, if students have learned that examination questions are taken only from classroom content, they may pay little attention to reading assignments. Other areas that affect attention and selection are current priorities and the usefulness and meaningfulness of new material. Selectivity is also influenced by numbers of items and the complexity of tasks or sources. For example, it is harder to pay attention to several people talking than it is to one, and it is easier to pay attention to several simple stimuli or simultaneously perform more than one simple task than if either are complex (Leahey and Harris, 1989).

An initial encoding process begins after information is selected. Ormrod (1990) points out that each new piece of information takes about ten seconds to encode. Multiple propositions (units of knowledge concerning relationships between objects or events) are presented during each class meeting. Given the time necessary for encoding, learners can process very few propositions per class. Therefore, instructors can help learners select important information by highlighting it, building on redundancy, connecting it to previous information, or simply telling students what is important.

Automaticity, or automatic processing, occurs with little or no conscious effort or allocation of attention. These processes can be executed simultaneously with other cognitive processes and activities. *Controlled processes*, on the other hand, must be executed serially because they require so much attention. As controlled tasks become habitual, they may eventually become automatic (Leahey and Harris, 1989). Many academic tasks, such as reading, writing, and number usage, require the performance of simultaneous subtasks. Comprehension, for instance, is a controlled process that demands the automatic occurrence of word recognition, Many basic tasks and skills should not require the degree of attention that will distract learners from focusing on more critical information. Repetition and practice of tasks (letter and word identification, basic mathematical procedures) enable learners to read for comprehension or interpret statistical problems. Learners may use different modalities (such as auditory or visual approaches) to achieve mastery of foundational information.

Short-Term, or Working, Memory. The limited capacity of short-term memory is about seven, plus or minus two, bits or chunks of information at one time (Miller, 1956). *Chunking,* or combining bits of information, allows them to take up less space in working memory. "Since the memory span is a fixed number of chunks, we can increase the number of bits of information that it contains simply by building larger and larger chunks, each chunk containing more information than before" (Miller, 1956, p. 93). An example of chunking is the use of an encoding mnemonic, or mental cue, to remember the spelling of certain types of words ("i before e except after c").

Another process that occurs in short-term memory is *rehearsal. Maintenance rehearsal* holds information long enough for some action to occur, then the information disappears. For instance, repeating the digits of a phone number from the time it is looked up until the dialing is completed or repeating a formula used in accounting until it can be used in an examination keeps the memory alive as long as it is needed. *Elaborative rehearsal* is a process that helps transfer new information to long-term memory by relating it to other concepts already in storage and developing new associations among those concepts (Leahey and Harris, 1989). Specific discussion of the use of elaboration as a technique will occur in the next section of this chapter.

The processes described in sensory and short-term memory must occur before material is encoded in long-term memory. New information must be attended to, selected, and passed on to working memory for initial processing (Leahey and Harris, 1989). In working memory, the information undergoes further processing and beginning integration with existing memory stores before moving on to the third component, long-term memory.

Long-Term Memory. Long-term memory not only provides a mechanism for storing information over time, it also provides a knowledge base from which to interpret new information. All new information is related to or associated with previously known entities. As a result, the same information will be stored differently by different persons because the information already stored in their respective memories is not the same (Ormrod, 1990).

Encoding refers to a variety of processes that put information into storage in an appropriate form for later use, and the kind of encoding that occurs makes a major difference in how much is later remembered. These processes happen automatically as individuals perceive, think, and act, and they are biased toward meaning, toward the most important ideas in a scene or text, and toward context-relevant interpretations (Potter, 1990).

The first process, *verbal coding,* is used to store large amounts of information. People attach verbal labels to objects and events, often learn information in verbatim fashion, or use language to help them make associations (Ormrod, 1990).

A second process, *imagery,* is often used to encode information for storage. All the perceptual modalities (visual, auditory, tactile, kinesthetic, and olfactory) are used when storing images, because memory is a by-product of perceptual analysis. Concrete information (book, chalkboard, calculator) is typically remembered better than abstract or conceptual information (truth, health, liberty) because concrete words have readily available imagery (Leahey and Harris, 1989). Cognitive (mental) maps are image representations of places people are familiar with, and they use them to describe, to navigate, and to give directions to others. For instance, asking someone for directions to a specific site causes them to use their cognitive map to point out landmarks, street numbers, and right and left turns. Imagery is most often discussed in terms of visual examples, and individuals have remarkably accurate memories for visual information. However, visual images do not always provide a complete and accurate representation, so they may not be helpful when precise, detailed material needs to be stored. Despite this limitation, visual aids are widely used in the classroom because visual images can be quickly stored and retained over long periods of time (Ormrod, 1990).

Imagery also provides the foundation for *mnemonics,* strategies for more efficient encoding. Learners may use a variety of mnemonic strategies, such as making up a song to help remember something or imposing meaning on a fixed series of items (using "On Old Olympus's Timbered Tops a Finn and German Viewed Some Hops" to remember the correct order and number of spinal nerves). Another strategy is to invent a method of loci that provides associations between items such as steps of a procedure and images (linking steps in using a new computer to rooms in one's house and objects in those rooms by creating bizarre images). Mnemonics are valuable because they impose organization on material and increase its meaningfulness. Mnemonics are helpful in learning arbitrary, verbatim information where elements are not particularly associated with other elements or where a specific order must be learned. They also take advantage of our natural information-processing tendency to impose structure and organization on material that we process (Leahey and Harris, 1989). It seems that everyone stores information the way it was encoded; however, each person stores material in relation to what is already individually known.

Using verbal coding and imagery and establishing meaning are ways of storing what is called *declarative knowledge,* or knowledge of facts and information. Individuals also need to have *procedural knowledge,* or knowledge of how to perform skills or do tasks. Procedural memories can be established only by performing or practicing a response, and it is this response, not information about it, that is retrieved (Boss, 1986). While some behaviors may be encoded using the preceding processes, to actually perform behaviors successfully, persons must be able to adapt to changing conditions.

Anderson (1976) identifies codes, known as *productions,* that allow persons to respond to different conditions in the environment. Productions are basically if-then rules wherein the "if" part specifies the condition under which a particular behavior will occur, and the "then" part specifies what the behavior will be. For instance, productions for using certain computer software would include rules such as "If I want to exit the program, then I use the

F7 function key," or "If I want to review content, then I use the up or down arrow keys."

After encoding, specific processes may be used to *store,* or retain, new information. Ormrod (1990) offers the following principles of long-term memory storage: (1) some pieces of information are selected and others are excluded; (2) underlying meanings are more likely to be stored than verbatim input; (3) existing knowledge about the world is used to understand new information; and (4) some existing knowledge may be added to new information, so what is learned may be more than, or different from, the information actually presented.

Elaborative rehearsal facilitates storage in long-term memory. *Elaboration* is a process of learning more than the new information, because it uses both new and existing knowledge to construct a meaningful interpretation of the new content. Therefore, instructors need to consider that different individuals elaborate the same information in different ways and accordingly learn different things (Ormrod, 1990). Elaboration sometimes creates distorted or erroneous information when the new material is altered to fit the individual's preconceived notions about the world. Because of this, merely presenting information to learners does not correct their erroneous beliefs. Despite potential distortions of information, elaborated material is more effectively learned and retained than nonelaborated information, and most elaborations reflect correct assumptions and interpretations of events. Learners should be taught and encouraged to use elaboration strategies such as making inferences (deriving conclusions that are not explicit in what is written or spoken), finding analogies (the operation of a computer is analogous to the function of the human brain) and metaphors (whole-brain education), and constructing mental images. Elaboration may also be facilitated by the use of multimedia technologies such as intelligent tutorial systems and compact interactive discs that offer individualized training and instruction (Smith, 1990).

Although there is no single theory of adult learning, most writers suggest that adults want meaningful learning experiences. Some adults may be seeking to immediately apply new knowledge, others, to enhance proficiency and improve performance, and still others, to alter existing ineffective response patterns. Whatever the motivation for learning, adults enter the process with a rich reservoir of knowledge and experience.

The process of *meaningful learning* appears to facilitate both storage and retrieval because it associates new information with existing information in long-term memory. Ormrod (1990) describes meaningful learning as the process of placing, or subsuming, new information under an appropriate superordinate category. The author points out that meaningful learning is most likely to occur when learners (1) know they will be expected to explain new information later in their own words, (2) have a large body of knowledge already stored in long-term memory so there are more ideas to which new experiences can be related, and (3) are aware that a piece of previously learned information is related to a new piece of information and have both pieces in short-term memory at the same time. Meaningful learning, or comprehension, can be enhanced by relating new information to one's self or by relating new information to already familiar ideas and concepts.

Internal *organization* that occurs as new material is learned and stored ultimately helps facilitate retrieval of information from long-term memory. Instructors and trainers should present information in a highly organized manner by pointing out specific organizational schemes (using general introductions to new content and providing outlines of new information), providing organizational cues (such as category labels), and encouraging use of these cues for encoding and retrieval. Comparative organization schemes show students how new material relates to previous information or experiences, and aid in external organization of material. These techniques facilitate the internal organization of new material along with existing knowledge in long-term memory.

Retrieval, a process intimately related to encoding and organization, is determined by measures that fall into two general categories: recall and recognition. Bolles (1988, p. 47) says that "recall is the internal, automatic power of memory to produce an association." In *free recall,* such as an essay question that offers no cues, there are no hints to help people remember the desired or requested information. *Cued recall* is generally easier because there is some type of clue present to aid in retrieval. This retrieval cue may be a word, sight, odor, sound, or texture that reminds the learner of the information being sought. Cued recall depends on encoding specificity, so that the most effective cues during recall are the same as those encoded during learning (Bellezza, 1987). *Recognition,* on the other hand, is outward looking; it perceives the circumstances and context of an experience. *Yes-no recognition* presents some item and asks the learner to indicate whether or not the item is remembered. *Forced-choice recognition,* best exemplified by the multiple-choice test, requires the learner to choose the one correct answer from among several choices. Bolles (1986) points out that although it may be easier to recognize a fact than to recall one, if a person knows many facts about something, it takes longer to recognize any single one. Generally, recall and recognition work together, with effective encoding the best way to ensure effective retrieval.

Lavigne and Finley (1990) reviewed selected studies involving memory research with middle-aged adults. They suggested that adults may have retrieval facilitated by the following measures: (1) ample time should be allowed for retrieval tasks such as examinations; (2) multiple-choice questions should be incorporated in some portion of examinations, because the fewest age differences have been shown in recognition tasks; (3) it is helpful to craft essay questions to include multiple cues, since the greatest declines are on free-recall tasks; (4) encoding/retrieval cues (for instance, mnemonics)

Table 4.1. Application of Memory Processes
to Teaching and Learning

	Memory Process	Application
Sensory memory	Visual images	Use transparencies, chalkboard, written outlines
	Attention	Use large letters, bright colors, loud noises, emotionally strong stimuli
	Selection	Emphasize task simplicity (simple to complex); tell students what is important; use highlighting, redundancy
Short-term memory	Chunking	Use mnemonic devices to reduce information size
	Maintenance rehearsal	Repeat information until no longer needed
Long-term memory	Encoding	
	Verbal	Use object labels, verbatim learning, associations
	Imagery	Incorporate cognitive maps, visual aids, mnemonics
	Productions	Use practice responses, if-then rules
	Elaboration	Utilize inferences, metaphors, analogies, mental images
	Meaningful learning	Relate new information to already-existing concepts, ideas, knowledge
	Organization	Use outlines, category labels; relate new content to old content
	Retrieving	
	Free recall	No cues are offered
	Cued recall	Use word, sight, sound, odor, or texture to stimulate recall
	Yes-no recognition	Rely on true-false questions
	Forced-choice recognition	Utilize multiple-choice questions

should be provided as material is presented; and (5) both visual aids and verbal labeling can be employed to enhance learning.

Conclusion

The most prevalent view of memory structure, the Atkinson-Shiffrin model, proposes three distinct components: sensory memory, short-term memory, and long-term memory. A variety of mental activities have been conceived to account for the way information is processed in memory, with the three most common being encoding, storage, and retrieval. Current knowledge about memory functions has come primarily from laboratory-based research that used cross-sectional designs in which the performance of young and old adults was compared. It has been questioned whether the outcomes of those studies, generally unfavorable to older adults, reflected age and cohort differences or age changes. Growing numbers of researchers have found fewer age-related declines when memory was studied in the context of everyday adult lives.

The processing operations of cognition and memory were explored by organizing them under the three components of the structural model of memory. Suggested ways of applying the processing operations in teaching and learning were made as each component was discussed. Table 4.1 presents a summary of these suggestions.

The concept that memory and learning are different sides of the same coin is evident in the use of similar, and even the same, terminology when both are discussed. Learning strategies and memory strategies appear to be one and the same in terms of processing functions. The link with perceptual modalities is evident in techniques used to enhance attention and selection and in the use of imagery to encode information. Do successful learners have good memories? Are persons with good memories successful learners? I leave the reader with this thought by Bolles (1988, p. 23): "We remember what we understand; we understand only what we pay attention to; we pay attention to what we want."

References

Anderson, J. *Language, Memory, and Thought*. Hillsdale, N.J.: Erlbaum, 1976.

Atkinson, R., and Shiffrin, R. "Human Memory: A Proposed System and Its Control Processes." In K. Spence and J. Spence (eds.), *The Psychology of Learning and Motivation: Advances in Research and Theory*. Vol. 2. New York: Academic Press, 1968.

Baddeley, A. "Finding the Bloody Horse." In L. Poon, D. Rubin, and B. Wilson (eds.), *Everyday Cognition in Adulthood and Late Life*. Cambridge, England: Cambridge University Press, 1989.

Bahrick, H. "The Laboratory and Ecology: Supplementing Sources of Data for Memory Research." In L. Poon, D. Rubin, and B. Wilson (eds.), *Everyday Cognition in Adulthood and Late Life*. Cambridge, England: Cambridge University Press, 1989.

Bellezza, F. "Mnemonic Devices and Memory Schemas." In M. McDaniel and M. Pressley (eds.), *Imagery and Related Mnemonic Processes*. New York: Springer-Verlag, 1987.

Bolles, E. *Remembering and Forgetting*. New York: Walker, 1988.

Bootzin, R., Loftus, E., and Zajonc, R. *Psychology Today*. (5th ed.) New York: Random House, 1983.

Boss, B. "The Neurological and Neurophysiological Basis of Learning." *Journal of Neuroscience Nursing*, 1986, *18* (5), 256–264.

Botwinick, J. *Aging and Behavior*. (3rd ed.) New York: Springer, 1984.

Craik, F. "Age Differences in Human Memory." In J. Birren and K. W. Schaie (eds.), *Handbook of the Psychology of Aging*. New York: Van Nostrand Reinhold, 1977.

Gregg, V. *Introduction to Human Memory*. London: Routledge & Kegan Paul, 1986.

Hayslip, B., and Panek, P. *Adult Development and Aging*. New York: HarperCollins, 1989.

Hoffman, R., Bringman, W., Bamberg, M., and Klein, R. "Some Historical Observations on Ebbinghaus." In D. Gorfein and R. Hoffman (eds.), *Memory and Learning: The Ebbinghaus Centennial Conference*. Hillsdale, N.J.: Erlbaum, 1987.

Landauer, T. "Some Bad and Some Good Reasons for Studying Memory and Cognition in the Wild." In L. Poon, D. Rubin, and B. Wilson (eds.), *Everyday Cognition in Adulthood and Late Life*. Cambridge, England: Cambridge University Press, 1989.

Lapp, D. *Don't Forget: Easy Exercises for a Better Memory at Any Age*. New York: McGraw-Hill, 1987.

Lavigne, V., and Finley, G. "Memory in Middle-Aged Adults." *Educational Gerontology*, 1990, *16*, 447–461.

Leahey, T., and Harris, R. *Human Learning*. Englewood Cliffs, N.J.: Prentice Hall, 1989.

Long, H. *Adult Learning: Research and Practice*. New York: Cambridge University Press, 1983.

Merriam, S. B., and Caffarella, R. S. *Learning in Adulthood: A Comprehensive Guide*. San Francisco: Jossey-Bass, 1991.

Miller, G. "The Magical Number Seven, Plus or Minus Two: Some Limits on Our Capacity for Processing Information." *Psychological Review*, 1956, *63*, 81–97.

Ormrod, J. *Human Learning Principles, Theories, and Educational Applications*. Columbus, Ohio: Merrill, 1990.

Peterson, D. A. *Facilitating Education for Older Learners*. San Francisco: Jossey-Bass, 1983.

Poon, L. "Differences in Human Memory with Aging." In J. Birren and K. W. Schaie (eds.), *Handbook of the Psychology of Aging*. New York: Van Nostrand Reinhold, 1985.

Potter, M. "Remembering." In D. Osherson and E. Smith (eds.), *Thinking: An Invitation to Cognitive Science*. Vol. 3. Cambridge, Mass.: MIT Press, 1990.

Rybash, J., Hoyer, W., and Roodin, P. *Adult Cognition and Aging*. Elmsford, N.Y.: Pergamon Press, 1986.

Salthouse, T. *Adult Cognition: An Experimental Psychology of Human Aging*. New York: Springer-Verlag, 1982.

Salthouse, T. *Theoretical Perspectives on Cognitive Aging*. Hillsdale, N.J.: Erlbaum, 1991.

Schaie, K. W., and Geiwitz, J. *Adult Development and Aging*. Boston: Little, Brown, 1982.

Schaie, K. W., and Willis, S. *Adult Development and Aging*. (2nd ed.) Boston: Little, Brown, 1986.

Smith, R. M., and Associates. *Learning to Learn Across the Life Span*. San Francisco: Jossey-Bass, 1990.

KAY L. HUBER is associate professor of nursing at Messiah College, Grantham, Pennsylvania.

Learning-style instruments have specific purposes and certain limitations.

Review and Critique of Available Learning-Style Instruments for Adults

Waynne B. James, William E. Blank

Anyone who thoughtfully examines the learning process—particularly in adults—would conclude that it is, indeed, an extremely complex process. Although a considerable amount of research has been conducted on the dynamics of learning, we are only beginning to understand it. Researchers have attempted to identify and analyze many of the factors that appear to contribute to or inhibit efficient and effective learning. Much of this research has focused on elements external to the learner, such as the classroom setting, teaching methods and media, curriculum, and so on. Although less research has been conducted on elements internal to the learner, such as how the learner perceives, processes, interprets, stores, and recalls stimuli, many feel these elements are just as important, if not more so, in explaining and ultimately improving learning. The ways individual learners react to the overall learning environment and its various elements are often said to make up the learner's *learning style.*

One of the challenges the learning styles field is facing is the lack of widely agreed-on terminology. The concept of how learners react to their learning environment is most often referred to as either *learning style* or *cognitive style.* A good case can be made for either label; however, *learning style* seems to be taking hold. Keefe (1987) points out that *learning style* and *cognitive style* have often been used synonymously in the literature, although they decidedly are not the same. *Learning style* is the broader term and includes cognitive, affective, and physiological styles. We favor *learning style* over *cognitive style* because, like Keefe, we believe it is a broader term encompassing the entire learning process. We define *learning style* as the complex manner in which, and conditions under which, learners most efficiently and most effectively perceive, process, store, and recall what they are attempting to learn.

Learning-Style Dimensions

Before looking at instruments available for assessing the learning style of adults, we need to first establish a framework or taxonomy to use as a structure to assist in selecting and evaluating instruments for possible use. Most would agree that one of the important characteristics of any instrument—including a learning-style instrument—is that it should measure what it is supposed to measure. What are the various dimensions of learning style that instruments purport to measure? As with the definition of *learning style*, there is no universally accepted taxonomy of learning-style dimensions. But a taxonomy that is gaining in use is one that focuses on three major dimensions: information processing (cognitive), affective (for instance, personality), and physiological (for example, tolerance for noise, time-of-day rhythms).

Keefe (1987) describes each of the three dimensions of learning style. Cognitive styles, considered in Chapter Two, are information processing habits representing the learner's typical mode of perceiving, thinking, problem solving, and remembering. Each learner has preferred ways of perception, organization, and retention that are distinctive and consistent; these are cognitive styles. Affective styles, considered in Chapter Three, encompass aspects of personality that have to do with attention, emotion, and valuing. Affective learning styles are the learner's typical mode of arousing, directing, and sustaining behavior. We cannot directly observe affective learning style; we can only infer it from the learner's interaction with the environment. Physiological styles, according to Keefe (1987, p. 13), are "biologically-based modes of response that are founded on accustomed reaction to the physical environment, sex-related differences, and personal nutrition and health."

As adult education and training practitioners consider learning-style instruments for possible use, it is necessary to keep in mind these three broad dimensions of style: *information processing, affective,* and *physiological*. Practitioners should determine what is to be measured and locate an instrument that measures it. For example, trainers interested in determining the social setting in which potential trainees prefer to learn—that is, whether they prefer to work alone, with a partner, in a group, for example—should first recognize that they are dealing with the affective dimension of learning styles. But adult basic education teachers who want to find out more about which teaching methods and media would be most appropriate for their students are concerned with the cognitive dimension. Of course, practitioners should keep in mind that they may often be seeking answers to questions cutting across two or even all three dimensions. Even if they are interested in only one dimension, many learning-style instruments involve two or three.

Factors to Consider When Selecting Instruments

Selection of a particular learning-style instrument hinges on several factors. First of these is determining the intended use of the data to be collected from learners using the instrument. The next step is to determine what instruments are available that match the intended purpose and then to evaluate or critique potential instruments. Finally, an instrument is selected and utilized. How should adult educators go about the critical second step, reviewing and selecting learning-style instruments for a particular use?

We suggest that evaluation and eventual selection of a learning-style instrument should depend on three major criteria. These criteria include the appropriateness and soundness of the *conceptual base,* or theoretical underpinnings on which the instrument was developed, the *research data* supporting the instrument's soundness and usefulness, and, finally, *practical considerations* that determine the feasibility of using a particular instrument in a particular setting. All three criteria are crucial in determining which instrument might be appropriate for a particular purpose.

Conceptual Base. An instrument's conceptual or theoretical base can be determined by a careful examination of its title, stated purpose, subscale titles, and intended audience. If possible, the technical manual accompanying the instrument should be examined to determine the constructs used to develop the instrument and that it purports to measure. There are times when this information is not available from the technical manual. Practitioners should get in touch with the developer of the instrument and can also review journal articles reporting on the results of using that particular instrument. Often the literature will present a more balanced and objective evaluation of an instrument than the developer or technical manual will.

An important step in examining the conceptual base of an instrument is to consider questions such as the following that pertain to the intended use of the instrument. First, the kind of information being collected must be determined; what do the authors or publishers state will be the nature and purpose of the resulting information? Does the instrument address information processing, personality factors, or perceptual learning—or all of these? Second, the kinds of decisions or judgments that can be based on the results of the instrument depend on its intended use. Administering an instrument merely to meet administrative or legal mandates is not a wise use of time or money. Finally, a related issue concerns the theoretical underpinnings of the instrument. Do they match what practitioners are trying to measure and ultimately improve?

Research Data. Whether the instrument under consideration is effective and appropriate also depends on the information provided with respect to validity, reliability, and norms.

Validity. As a measurement concept, validity encompasses the appropriateness, meaningfulness, and usefulness of inferences made from test scores. It involves the use of evaluative judgments based on empirical evidence to bolster the adequacy and appropriateness of the inferences made (Messick, 1989). Test developers and measurement specialists believe that the validity of an instrument is the most crucial aspect to consider when evaluating its appropriateness. Since the process of validation entails much data accumulation to provide evidence that the instrument measures what it purports to measure, different conclusions need different types of evidence to support validity. Validity is not a single dimension, but rather a composite of measures that can be supported through quality research and test development efforts.

Dimensions often cited in discussions of these issues include the following: content, concurrent, predictive, and construct validity. Content validity refers to the degree of relevance and representativeness of the material on the assessment instrument. Concurrent validity considers whether a particular instrument is similar to other instruments measuring the same thing. Predictive validity considers the extent to which the instrument can anticipate what will happen at some future time based on an individual's current responses. Construct validity speaks to the underlying foundational aspects of a trait (or construct). Messick (1989) believes that construct validity is the only type of validity that needs to be considered, since it subsumes all the other forms.

Reliability. Reliability is determined by whether the results of an instrument remain the same over time and can be measured in several alternative formats—test/retest (administering an instrument on two occasions to the same individuals with a time interval in between), internal consistency (comparing patterns of responses based on specific formulas), consistency between forms, and consistency among administrators.

Norms. Norms are established to provide standards of comparison so that one individual's scores can be viewed as similar or dissimilar to the scores of others. This ideally includes consideration of the characteristics of the population sampled. Such characteristics can include age, gender, race and ethnicity, socioeconomic status, education level, and so on. In the literature, test/retest and internal consistency are the most often cited measures of reliability of learning-style instruments.

Practical Considerations. Following are some of the more practical considerations to keep in mind when evaluating learning-style instruments for possible use in a particular setting with a particular target group.

Physical Characteristics. Among the important considerations in evaluating learning-style instruments are the physical characteristics of the instrument itself. Physical characteristics include the instrument's overall appearance, page size, number of pages, whether there is a separate answer sheet, whether it includes self-carboning pages, the instrument's attractiveness, binding, clarity and size of print, and related factors.

Cost. Cost is an important consideration, especially if an instrument will be administered to a large number of learners or clients. Typical costs range from no charge, for those instruments in the public domain, to several dollars per copy for some proprietary instruments. Related concerns include minimum number of copies that can be ordered, whether the instrument must be ordered in multiples of twenty-five, fifty, or some other quantity, and whether related materials must be ordered in addition to the instruments.

Administration. The mechanics of administering the instruments to learners or clients must also be considered. Instruments that are difficult to administer may yield questionable results due to difficulties with simply getting the instruments into the hands of respondents and making sure they understand how to complete them. Administrative factors include whether the instructions are clear, whether a test administrator is needed, how many sheets are involved, how many test booklets or other forms are needed for each learner, whether media or related equipment is necessary (for example, slide projector or computer), and whether the instrument can be group administered versus individually administered.

Scoring and Interpretation. These are important considerations to keep in mind when selecting instruments. Scoring concerns include whether the instruments can be scored immediately locally or whether they must be sent to another location and, if so, what the cost and turnaround time are. If they can be scored locally, can they be self-scored or must a test administrator do it? Another factor is whether any special training or certification is required for someone to score the instruments. Interpretation of scores is an additional concern. Can respondents interpret their own score with information made available to them, or must a trained test administrator provide the interpretation? If the latter, how involved and time-consuming is the interpretation process?

Documentation. Some potentially useful instruments end up being of limited use because they are not accompanied by sufficient or accurate documentation. This documentation may include an administrator's guide, a technical manual, and other materials. Well-documented instruments come with comprehensive documentation, including validity and reliability data, an explanation of norms, information on the theoretical or conceptual bases of the instruments, and addresses of people to contact in order to arrange test administration, scoring, and interpretation. Documentation available for the instruments reviewed in this article ranged from nonexistent to excellent.

Description and Critique of Learning-Style Instruments

In this section, we present some basic information and a brief critique of selected learning-style instruments. The instruments reviewed include all three of the major dimensions discussed earlier—perceptual modalities, information processing, and personality factors. A brief description of each instrument with a bibliographical citation follows. Table 5.1 includes useful details on selected instruments.

Table 5.1. Critique of Selected Learning-Style Instruments

Learning-Style Instrument	Dimension(s)[a] I	M	P	Number of Subscales	Developed for Adults?	Adult Norms Available?	Evidence of Validity?[b]	Evidence of Reliability?[b]	Strength of Research Base[b]	Cost[c] per Instrument	Overall Instrument Usability[b]	Comments
Barbe-Milone	X			3	Yes	No	1	1	1	P.D.	3	Only ten items
MMPALT II	X			7	Yes	No	2	3	2	not avail.	1	Time consuming
Swassing-Barbe	X			3	No	No	1	2	2	avail. as kit	1	Time consuming
Grasha-Riechmann			X	6	Yes	Yes	2	3	3	2	3	Widely used
Gregorc	X			4	Yes	Yes	2	2	2	2	3	In wide use
Hemispheric Mode Indicator	X			1	Yes	Yes	2	2	2	2	3	Easy use and scoring
Herrmann	X			4	Yes	Yes	3	?	3	3	2	Expensive
Kolb	X			4	Yes	Yes	1	2	2	2	3	Widely used
Schmeck	X			14	Yes	Yes	3	3	2	not avail.	2	Sent off for scoring
Witkin	X			1	Yes	Yes	2	2	3	2	3	For research only
Canfield	X	X	X	17	Yes	Yes	2	3	2	3	2	Alternate formats available
Honey and Mumford	X			4	Yes	Yes	2	2	2	3	3	Easy to use; costly
Keirsey	X		X	4	Yes	Yes	2	0	2	1	3	Based on Myers-Briggs
Myers-Briggs	X		X	4	Yes	Yes	3	3	3	2	2	Training required for use
Silver-Hanson LSI	X		X	4	Yes	Yes	2	2	3	2	3	Based on Jung typology
Sternberg	X			13	Yes	Yes	2	2	2	1	2	Complex; lengthy; recent
CITE	X	X	X	9	No	No	1	1	2	P.D.	3	Comprehensive version available
PEPS	X	X	X	20	Yes	Yes	2	2	3	2	2	Sent off for scoring
Hill	X	X	X	28	Yes	No	1	1	2	P.D.	1	Highly complex
NASSP	X	X	X	24	No	No	2	0	3	2	1	Rigorously developed

[a]Dimensions: I = information processing; M = perceptual modality; P = personality.

[b]Validity/reliability/research base/usability: 0 = unable to determine; 1 = low, weak; 2 = moderate; 3 = strong.

[c]Cost: P.D. = public domain; 1 = $1.00 or less per copy; 2 = $1.01–$5.00 per copy; 3 = over $5.00 per copy.

Perceptual Modality

Barbe-Milone Modality Checklist (Barbe and Milone, 1980) consists of ten sets
of three statements asking individuals to check the one "most like" them.

Multi Modal Paired Associates Learning Test–Revised (MMPALT II) was revised
by Cherry (1981) based on a previous version developed by French
(1975a, 1975b) and Gilley (1975). It consists of seven performance-
based subtests of ten items, each covering seven sensory modalities.

Swassing-Barbe Modality Index (Barbe and Swassing, 1988) is also a performance-based instrument testing recall of sensory data within three modalities.

Information Processing

Grasha-Riechmann's Student Learning Style Scales (Hruska and Grasha, 1982)
consist of sixty self-report Likert statements.

Gregorc's Style Delineator (Gregorc, 1982) is a self-report instrument that includes ten sets of four items that must be rank ordered.

Hemispheric Mode Indicator (McCarthy, 1986) consists of thirty-two pairs of
bipolar statements rated on a Likert scale.

Herrmann's Brain Dominance Inventory (Herrmann, 1990) is a self-report instrument using a variety of different formats to obtain scores on the seven
subscales.

Kolb's Learning Style Inventory (Kolb, 1985) involves rank ordering four
choices within twelve sets of statements.

Schmeck's Inventory of Learning Processes (Schmeck, Geisler-Brenstein, and
Cercy, 1991) involves sixty-two true-false statements.

Witkin's Group Embedded Figures Test (Oltman, Raskin, and Witkin, 1971) is
a perceptual test of ability to match simple designs within twenty-five
more complex figures.

Personality Factors

Canfield's Learning Styles Inventory (Canfield, 1988) consists of a set of thirty
clusters of four self-report statements that must be rank ordered.

Honey and Mumford's Learning Styles Questionnaire (Honey and Mumford,
1989) includes eighty self-report agree-disagree statements.

Keirsey Temperament Sorter (Keirsey and Bates, 1984) involves seventy bipolar self-report items.

Myers-Briggs Type Indicator (Briggs and Myers, 1977) exists in several different forms; the most commonly used version consists of 126 bipolar items.

Silver and Hanson's Teaching, Learning, and Curriculum Model serves as the
basis for several instruments for both teachers and students: *Learning
Preference Inventory* (Silver and Hanson, 1978), *Learning Style Inventory*
(Silver and Hanson, 1980a), and *Teaching Style Inventory* (Silver and
Hanson, 1980b). The Learning Style Inventory includes thirty sets of
four self-description items that must be ranked in order of preference.

Sternberg's Thinking Styles Questionnaire (Sternberg and Wagner, 1991) includes 104 self-report strategies related to thinking skills, rated on a
Likert scale.

Combination Instruments

Center for Innovative Teaching Experiences (CITE) Learning Styles Instrument
(Babich and Randol, 1976) is a self-report instrument of forty-five items.

Dunn, Dunn, and Price's *Productivity Environmental Preference Survey (PEPS)*
(Dunn, Dunn, and Price, 1988) consists of 100 Likert-scale self-report
items.

Hill's *Cognitive Style Mapping* (Hill, 1977; Nunney, 1978) involves a self-
report Likert response system of 224 items.

National Association for Secondary School Principals' *Learning Style Profile*
(Keefe and others, 1989) consists of 126 items of mixed format. Although originally intended for use with high school students, it appears
to have a solid research base, as discussed in Keefe and Monk (1990).

In our analysis of selected learning-style instruments, we subjected a variety of instruments to intensive scrutiny, considering both practicality and
research-based concerns. Using available information (which may have been
incomplete for some instruments), we compared selected instruments based
on the previously specified criteria. See Table 5.1 for our evaluation.

Research Results

This section presents a brief summary of representative research studies involving selected learning-style instruments. Research reviewed for this section included some conducted by other researchers as well as several studies
conducted by the authors and their doctoral students. One of the most important and troubling results of numerous research studies is that they often
fail to yield solid evidence that the construct of learning style truly exists.
Often, the results of various tests of reliability and validity are contradictory
or inconclusive. Also troubling is the fact that some of the instruments developed for use with children have been applied to adults without determining
whether this is appropriate. Bonham (1988) succinctly subtitled an article
"Let the Buyer Beware," indicating reservations about the appropriateness of
various instruments. However, some research does support cautious use of
the concept of learning style. Hannum and Hansen (1989, p. 119) concluded
that "unfortunately the research evidence on learning styles is quite mixed.
For all its intuitive appeal, it is rare to find clear examples of these styles that
significantly influence the ability of a person to learn when his/her style is not
attended to."

Since space is limited, only research involving perceptual modality (cognitive) instruments will be touched on; however, the reader should be reminded that this body of research is fairly representative of the research that
has been conducted in the other learning-style dimensions (affective and
physiological).

Instruments related to perceptual modalities show discrepant results.

Studies reported by the authors and others (James and Blank, 1991; James and Galbraith, 1985) support the use of the MMPALT II with adults. In an experimental study, Hutchison (1992) found that student learning performance (as measured on a written examination) was affected by perceptual dominance (as measured by the MMPALT II) in print and aural modalities. Grady (1992) administered four instruments, including MMPALT II, Barbe-Milone Modality Checklist, and CITE, to a sample of 100 adults in an attempt to address construct validity through a multitrait, multimethod process. Grady was unable to document construct validity, and two of the instruments (CITE and Barbe-Milone) failed to demonstrate suitable reliability for her specific population.

James and Blank (1993) calculated Pearson product moment correlations between a variety of subtests purporting to measure the same construct using a variety of instruments. Since the sample size was limited ($n = 26$), this investigation should be regarded as exploratory; equivalent subscale correlations need to be determined using larger numbers of subjects. But these data represent an initial attempt to address validity and reliability issues across a range of learning-style instruments for adults.

Pearson correlations between the Swassing-Barbe Modality Index perceptual modality subtest scores and the Dunn, Dunn, and Price PEPS corresponding scores were low: visual $r = 0.163$; auditory $r = -0.033$; tactile $r = -0.264$; kinesthetic $r = -0.133$. Correlations between the PEPS and the MMPALT II were also low and often negative: auditory $r = -0.056$; visual $r = -0.322$; tactile/haptic $r = 0.109$; intake/olfactory $r = -0.343$. Another study by Coolidge-Parker (1989) indicated a similar lack of correlation between these two instruments.

Correlations between the MMPALT II and the Swassing-Barbe (both performance-based instruments) correlated somewhat better with each other than either correlated with the PEPS (visual $r = 0.170$; aural $r = 0.451$; kinesthetic $r = 0.631$; visual/print $r = 0.251$; kinesthetic/haptic $r = 0.291$).

In summary, although various authors claim strong reliability and validity for their instruments, a solid research base for many of these claims does not exist.

Concerns and Cautions

Adult education practitioners and researchers should be cautioned about the use of existing learning-style instruments. Perhaps the most important caution is that, given the conflicting and inconclusive evidence regarding the validity and reliability of many instruments, it is imperative to use data derived from them with great care when making decisions regarding students and programs. These data should be treated as potentially useful—but not all-important—pieces of information in the decision-making process.

Other cautions include the following: avoid administering instruments to populations for which they were not developed or normed; use instruments specifically developed for special populations such as special needs learners; and be careful not to use results inappropriately. A final caution: Keep in mind whether an instrument is measuring true learning strength or predisposition or, rather, simply measuring preference.

Conclusion

It seems clear that the research related to various aspects of learning style and learning-style assessment has yielded mixed results. Continued research is warranted on all aspects of the topic. However, practitioners need to be cognizant of the limitations related to each particular instrument and should use the information obtained from instruments as an awareness tool rather than a research "truth." The selection of a particular learning-style assessment instrument depends on the identified need for such an instrument along with the support of an appropriate research base and practical considerations for use.

References

Babich, A. M., and Randol, P. "Learning Styles Inventory Reliability Report." Unpublished manuscript, Wichita Public Schools, Wichita, Kans., 1976.

Barbe, W. B., and Milone, M. N., Jr. "Modality." *Instructor*, 1980, *89*, 44–47.

Barbe, W. B., and Swassing, R. H. *Teaching Through Modality Strengths: Concepts and Practices.* Columbus, Ohio: Zaner-Bloser, 1988.

Bonham, L. A. "Learning Style Instruments: Let the Buyer Beware." *Lifelong Learning*, 1988, *11* (6), 12–16.

Briggs, K. C., and Myers, I. B. *Myers-Briggs Type Indicator*. Palo Alto, Calif.: Consulting Psychologists Press, 1977.

Canfield, A. A. *Canfield Learning Styles Inventory (LSI)*. Los Angeles: Western Psychological Services, 1988.

Cherry, C. E., Jr. "The Measurement of Adult Learning Styles: Perceptual Modality." Unpublished doctoral dissertation, Department of Curriculum and Instruction, University of Tennessee, 1981. (*Dissertation Abstracts International, 42*, 09A)

Coolidge-Parker, J. "A Comparison of Perceived and Objectively Measured Perceptual Learning Style Modality Elements of Court Reporters and Court Reporting Students." Unpublished doctoral dissertation, College of Education, University of South Florida, 1989.

Dunn, R., Dunn, K., and Price, G. E. *Productivity Environmental Preference Survey*. Lawrence, Kans.: Price Systems, Inc., 1988.

French, R. L. "Teaching Strategies and Learning." Unpublished manuscript, Department of Curriculum and Instruction, University of Tennessee, Knoxville, 1975a.

French, R. L. "Teaching Style and Instructional Strategy." Unpublished manuscript, Department of Curriculum and Instruction, University of Tennessee, Knoxville, 1975b.

Gilley, D. V. "Personal Learning Styles: Exploring the Individual's Sensory Input Processes." Unpublished doctoral dissertation, Department of Curriculum and Instruction, University of Tennessee, 1975. (*Dissertation Abstracts International, 36*, 08A)

Grady, L. B. "Convergent and Discriminant Validation of Four Instruments Assessing Perceptual Learning Styles Using a Multitrait-Multimethod Matrix Approach." Unpublished doctoral dissertation, College of Education, University of South Florida, 1992.

Gregorc, A. G. *An Adult's Guide to Style.* Maynard, Miss.: Gabriel Systems, 1982.

Hannum, W., and Hansen, C. *Instructional Systems Development in Large Organizations.* Englewood Cliffs, N.J.: Educational Technology Publications, 1989.

Herrmann, N. *The Creative Brain.* Lake Luree, N.C.: Brain Books, 1990.

Hill, J. E. *Cognitive Style Mapping.* Bloomfield Hills, Mich.: Oakland Community College, 1977.

Honey, P., and Mumford, A. *Learning Styles Questionnaire.* King of Prussia, Pa.: Organization Design and Development, 1989.

Hruska, S., Riechmann, S., and Grasha, A. F. "The Grasha-Riechmann Student Learning Style Scales." In J. W. Keefe (ed.), *Student Learning Styles and Brain Behavior.* Reston, Va.: National Association of Secondary School Principals, 1982.

Hutchison, S. W., Jr. "Dominant Perceptual Modality Element and Learning Performance: A Factorial Study." Unpublished doctoral dissertation, College of Education, University of South Florida, 1992.

James, W. B., and Blank, W. E. "A Comparison of Adults' Perceptual Learning Style and Their Educational Level." *Mountain Plains Adult Education Association Journal of Adult Education,* 1991, *19* (2), 11–21.

James, W. B., and Blank, W. E. "Correlations of Selected Learning Style Instruments." Unpublished data, Adult and Vocational Department, University of South Florida, 1993.

James, W. B., and Galbraith, M. W. "Perceptual Learning Styles: Implications and Techniques for the Practitioner." *Lifelong Learning,* 1985, *3* (2), 214–218.

Keefe, J. W. *Learning Style Theory and Practice.* Reston, Va.: National Association of Secondary School Principals, 1987.

Keefe, J. W., and Monk, J. S. *Learning Style Profile: Examiner's Manual.* Reston, Va.: National Association of Secondary School Principals, 1990.

Keefe, J. W., Monk, J. S., Letteri, C. A., Languis, M., and Dunn, R. *Learning Style Profile.* Reston, Va.: National Association of Secondary School Principals, 1989.

Keirsey, D., and Bates, M. *Please Understand Me: Character and Temperament Types.* Delmar, Calif.: Prometheus Nemesis Books, 1984.

Kolb, D. A. *Learning Style Inventory.* Boston: McBer, 1985.

McCarthy, B. *Hemispheric Mode Indicator: Right and Left Brain Approaches to Learning.* Barrington, Ill.: Excel, Inc., 1986.

Messick, S. "Validity." In R. L. Linn (ed.), *Educational Measurement.* New York: Macmillan, 1989.

Nunney, D. N. "Cognitive Style Mapping." *Training and Development Journal,* 1978, *32* (9), 50–57.

Oltman, P. K., Raskin, E., and Witkin, H. A. *Group Embedded Figures Test.* Palo Alto, Calif.: Consulting Psychologists Press, 1971.

Schmeck, R. R., Geisler-Brenstein, and Cercy, S. P. "Self-Concept and Learning: The Revised Inventory of Learning Processes." *Educational Psychology,* 1991, *11* (3 and 4), 343–362.

Silver, H. F., and Hanson, J. R. *Learning Preference and Inventory.* Moorestown, N.J.: Institute for Cognitive and Behavioral Studies, 1978.

Silver, H. F., and Hanson, J. R. *Learning Style Inventory.* Moorestown, N.J.: Institute for Cognitive and Behavioral Studies, 1980a.

Silver, H. F., and Hanson, J. R. *Teaching Style Inventory.* Moorestown, N.J.: Institute for Cognitive and Behavioral Studies, 1980b.

Sternberg, R. J., and Wagner, R. K. *MSG Thinking Styles Inventory.* Tallahassee, Fla.: Star Mountain Projects, Inc., 1991.

WAYNNE B. JAMES *is professor of adult and vocational education, University of South Florida.*

WILLIAM E. BLANK *is associate professor of adult and vocational education, University of South Florida.*

The fundamentals of learning how to learn are presented with examples of their application in adult and continuing education settings.

What Instructors Need to Know About Learning How to Learn

Catherine A. Stouch

The purpose of this chapter is to review the fundamentals of learning how to learn and to show how to apply them in adult and continuing education. "Learning how to learn involves possessing, or acquiring, the knowledge and skill to learn effectively in whatever learning situation one encounters" (Smith, 1982, p. 19). Instructors need to consciously incorporate learning how to learn in all teaching plans. Adults are individual learners with unique needs. Using the concepts of learning how to learn is one way to acknowledge learners' individual differences.

Three Components of the Learning-How-to-Learn Concept

Learning how to learn includes three components: knowledge about learning, knowledge about learning style, and skills to improve learning proficiency (Smith, 1982). The first component of learning how to learn is *knowledge about learning*. Students need general knowledge about learning, such as how memory operates; they also need self-awareness, for instance, of how they approach a reading assignment. To apply this knowledge, learners need skills for three common types of learning: self-directed learning, collaborative or group learning, and formal education. Applied examples for each type are included in this chapter.

The second component of learning how to learn is *knowledge about learning style*. When learners understand the attributes of their learning styles, they can seek out or ask for the instruction they need. Also, learning-style information gives learners the knowledge to try out some aspects of other learning styles, and thus potentially broadens the ways they learn.

The third component of learning how to learn is *skills to improve learning proficiency*. Every example in this chapter illustrates this component. Each time instructors incorporate learning-how-to-learn components into the curriculum, they are providing information and practice that increases their students' ability to learn that content as well as future content (Smith, 1982). For example, when a learner acquires the fundamentals of how to use the Microsoft Windows personal computer program, each subsequent Windows-based program is easier to learn and productivity in each comes more quickly. This is because the learner has learned how to learn in Windows. Windows has become a learning strategy, and the learner relies on that strategy as the foundation, to which he or she adds only the new skills and functions of each new Windows-based program.

Why Instructors Need to Know About Learning How to Learn

Learners have a set of strategies, "a plan of a sequence of actions to attain a learning objective" (Klauer, 1988, p. 11) for learning that are acquired through experience. They use these strategies to attack new learning. If the strategies are ineffective or less effective, learning will not occur or will occur more slowly. Thus, the recognition of learning strategies and the plan for teaching alternative strategies is central to cost-effective training. Business is rightly concerned about the cost-effectiveness of training. Therefore, business and learning how to learn are logical partners.

Any learning repertoire may have weaknesses. Adults have an array of strategies for learning skills and concepts. These strategies were learned in the past and are based on past learning challenges. But with the pace of change and the rapid aging of information, adults are regularly faced with learning for which they may have no effective strategies. Thus, learning how to learn is necessary to ensure continual learning.

For example, fast-track consultants at major management consulting companies have a lifetime of success experiences. As a result, they have acquired few strategies for learning from failures and mistakes. An executive in one such consulting company used the following strategy to help himself and his immediate staff learn from a failure experience. He wrote up the failure experience as a case study. Then the executive wrote a two-column description of a fictitious staff meeting to review the case. One column listed the script, like a movie script, of what this executive expected each person in the meeting would say. In the second column beside each scripted line, the executive wrote the thoughts and feelings he had but did not express as the scripted discussion progressed. The case and this script were shared with all staff involved with the failure experience and were then used as the basis for a discussion, bringing to light the unspoken feelings that naturally surround failure. Finally, as the discussion progressed, participants began to acknowledge ways they could have behaved differently. Possible strategies for avoiding similar failure in the future were identified. This strategy for learning from failure allowed everyone to reflect in a context where self-assessment was safe and thus increased the chances for participants to see and admit their roles in failure (Argyris, 1991).

Fundamentals of Learning How to Learn

Learning how to learn is a continual process, not a discrete event in a course (Smith, 1990b). What students already know about learning how to learn will contribute to their learning in a course. And what the teacher adds to their learning-how-to-learn repertoire will incrementally increase their ability to learn in all future learning settings (Smith, 1982).

Learning how to learn involves change. Learners must adapt or change the ways they have gone about learning, perhaps for years. Furthermore, learners must trust that the new learning will help them be successful. Like all the changes facing workers today, altering one's learning mechanisms is disruptive and uncomfortable at first and thus requires a safe, supportive environment as a backdrop (Smith, 1983).

Learning how to learn can be frustrating and hard work (Bunker, 1989). Patterns of learning are deeply ingrained. It takes time and concerted effort to add new patterns to the learning repertoire. So learning how to learn is tolerated best when related to previously encountered learning problems. "A learner who has struggled with an apathetic collaborative learning group will be more willing to work at learning strategies that energize such groups" (Smith, 1982, p. 140).

Learning how to learn delivers the most rewards after the fact. After gaining knowledge about how learning occurs, acquiring awareness of one's learning style, and learning the skills to improve one's learning efficiency, subsequent learning will be enhanced through the learner's active seeking and asking for the learning elements needed, if they are not provided.

In summary, instruction in learning how to learn must be beneficial enough to be worth the change effort on the learner's part and for the learner to engage in it and to gain benefits from it in future learning settings.

Teaching Generalizable Learning Strategies

Highly generalizable learning strategies may be taught as a first step toward more content-specific strategies. General learning-how-to-learn procedures—such as verbalizing the process used to understand and incorporate a new skill, or reflecting on one's learning style and how it can be used best in a new learning context—may be taught in any content-specific course. Once learned, such procedures can be used in any learning setting (Klauer, 1988).

Since learning strategies have varying levels of generality, instructors best serve their learners when they consider the content-specific learning strategies needed to learn course content. The typical workplace instructional design is composed of declarative knowledge (the "what" of the content), then procedural knowledge (the "how" of the content), followed by practice, followed by feedback. Learning how to learn is best incorporated between the declarative and procedural knowledge steps in the form of why this skill is important and when to use it, and with the practice step, in the form of practice on when and why to use the skill (Smith, 1990a). For example, in my workplace supervisory skills course, learners must acquire the most current information about performance appraisals. Research in a business school library is required. This library research has two purposes: to help learners learn to find current information germane to workplace needs, and to help them learn the newest information on performance appraisal. After the declarative knowledge of what performance appraisal is and what terms it relates to, the learners are introduced to some research concepts such as key words. They were also asked to explain why research skills are important to their future as supervisors. (This is a learning-how-to-learn method to build one's motivation by identifying one's own purpose for learning.) When research assignments were initiated, the practice phase of learning was filled with hands-on practice with a computerized card catalogue, CD-ROM topical indexes, Library of Congress keyword references, and the like. The practice gave each learner experience with when and why to use the research learning skills as well as with collecting sources on the assigned topic of performance appraisals. The hands-on learning about when each research source and skill is most useful builds learning how to learn into the practice phase of this class.

Care needs to be taken to present learning strategies as alternatives, not as singular, perfect tools. Although the instructor's analysis of the content to be learned may indicate that strategy A is ideal for acquisition of skill X, learners may already have in their repertoire a learning strategy superior to strategy A for learning skill X. This is particularly important to remember in light of the diversity of experience and learning styles adults bring to the learning environment (Klauer, 1988). For example, when teaching a new programming language to experienced programmers, I was reminded of preexisting learning strategies. I had taught the programming language to many nonprogrammers using a strategy that relied on general rules followed by examples of each. Once this content was understood, categories of programming commands were introduced, followed by examples and programming practice. This analytical strategy built from specific components to a unified whole. (See Chapter Two for further discussion of these particular strategies.)

However, when two experienced programmers were part of one class, I found they struck out on their own as soon as I discussed the general rules. Their strategy for learning this new programming language was to take the general rules and use them to decipher complete computer programs written in this language. Their preexisting learning strategy was to use a complete program in the new language and analyze it using their knowledge of what programs do plus a few general rules. This global strategy built from a whole to its components. They were just as productive using their learning strategy as other learners were with mine. My greatest gift to these experienced programmers was to get out of the way of their successful learning strategy.

As with any learning, learning strategies are only acquired and incorporated into long-term memory when adequately practiced (Klauer, 1988). (See Chapter Four for more on memory.) Learning-how-to-learn skills and ideas need immediate practice. Within any course, only one or two learning skills may be incorporated. But, within that course, the skills should be mentioned, explained, practiced, checked, reinforced, and repeated just as any other course component should be.

Before considering content-specific skills in learning how to learn, it must be noted that learning strategies are but one piece of the environment within which learning occurs. In addition, prior knowledge, intellectual capacity, motivation, and instructional and situational factors must be supportive to learning as well as learning how to learn (Klauer, 1988; Hammond, 1990; Smith, 1982). In essence, learning how to learn is one piece of a well-designed learning experience.

Teaching Learning How to Learn as Part of Content Instruction

Several approaches to teaching learning how to learn should be mentioned.

Techniques for Institutional Learning. Institutional learning refers to formal coursework in schools and colleges that are part of our traditional education system (Gibbons, 1990). Success in institutional environments requires structured skills for absorbing, retaining, and recalling course content. Learning how to learn in these environments is somewhat akin to acquiring good study skills.

Course-specific study skills, taught as part of any course, can enhance learner success in that course. Instructors can increase analytical skills in a history course by asking students to classify events into their own categories. Then they can ask students to infer the rules that define each category. Finally, the category-rule strategy can be applied to historical categories defined by the instructor or text. By seeing the process, students gain facility with acquiring someone else's categories and rules (Cunningham, 1983).

Another course-specific skill germane to many courses is the skill of recognizing the scope of the subject and how it changes over time. This skill aids a student in evaluating sources of information on the subject and determining when and how to disregard or replace subject matter (Smith, 1982). Understanding the scope of algebra and its relative stability over time will give credence to textbooks and parents with twenty-five-year-old knowledge. Or understanding the scope of management science and its constant updating will allow a student to place a ten-year-old article from the *Harvard Business Review* in its historical context.

Test taking can be taught as a learning-how-to-learn strategy. Test anxiety may detract from a student's grade. But gaining practice in exam situations can reduce that anxiety and increase performance. Course instructors can give students assignments throughout the course that share the same format and structure as the course's exams. Discussing performance on these assignments helps students develop exam skills. Sharing tips for clarifying an essay test response encourages the development of exam response skills. Decoding exam questions together with students helps them grasp the meanings of these questions.

Some strategies can be introduced early in the course to increase student reflection on these strategies (Smith, 1982). Active reading can be explained and contrasted with the students' current reading method. Once active reading's components (survey the assignment, formulate questions of interest, read for answers to questions, review what one just read, make selective notes from the reading) are practiced in class, students can readily compare it to their old reading method. Instructors can encourage active reading by asking students to review the upcoming assignment in class and to offer questions they hope will be answered by the assignment. At the next class, instructors can ask for points of interest and main ideas from the assigned reading.

Note taking is another learning strategy best addressed early in the course. After an hour of lecture, students can be asked to compare their note-taking methods with one another. Benefits of other methods can be collected, and suggestions for note taking can be shared based on the instructor's lecture style. For example, a lecturer who frequently gives numbered lists of points and expects them to be recalled in a specific order helps students by stating that this is expected. As a result of such note-taking activities, students learn specific strategies for organizing and relating content in this course. Yet they also learn that each course requires different note-taking methods for optimal performance. Both are strategies for learning how to learn in an institutional setting.

Learning-Style Information and Application. In many learning settings, learners become more effective after completing a learning-style assessment and understanding its uses. (See Chapter Five for more information on learning-style instruments.) When using an instrument to inform learners about their learning style, practitioners should consider three issues. First, the learner should be informed about how the instrument's author looks at learning. Second, the learning-style instrument should be used to create awareness of learning differences and of the value of those differences. Third, the learning-style information should be positioned as only the starting point for learners to study their behavior as learners (Merriam and Caffarella, 1991).

Learning-style knowledge may also aid learners in structuring a learning setting so the learner's preferences are balanced by others with complementary preferences. For example, a team manager may know she prefers to work alone and is focused on reaching many goals but build a team of people who prefer group processes and thus can help in reaching those shared goals (Bunker, 1989). Without such self-awareness, the team manager's preferences might have caused her to build a team of others who prefer to work alone with few goals in common. Such a team would exist in name only, dooming team production and the manager's hopes for reaching her many goals.

Independent Learning Projects. Learning how to learn is also applicable to independent learning. Two learning strategies needed in self-directed learning are how to find learning resources and how to narrow a topic of study to a manageable scope.

Finding learning resources may require nothing but a list to remind the independent learner of all the resources available. It may also entail finding learning resources in familiar settings to be used in independent ways (Merriam and Caffarella, 1991). For example, a common method for teaching adults to use computers is group verbal instruction accompanied by demonstration, followed by individual practice. However, one model for more effective instruction acknowledges that adults are often independent learners when using computers, trying new features in new situations to solve on-the-job needs. In one course I teach I give each student a list of hands-on problems to solve using the computer. Students may use whatever methods they wish to find the information that will help them solve the problems. Among the resources available to the students are on-line help, the program reference manuals, training manuals, trial-and-error experimentation in a safe environment, the instructor, and each other. After the course, most students report that this is one of the most beneficial parts of the course, since it gives them practice similar to the independent, on-the-job learning setting. Also, learners discover that learning resources masquerade in many forms: human, paper, and electronic. For learners familiar with their learning styles, this activity offers the chance to try something that stretches those styles. The visually oriented learner might try a discussion with another student as a way to solve one problem. A verbally oriented learner might try some visual trial-and-error with the built-in visual feedback of many computer systems. (See Chapter One on perceptual modalities.)

Narrowing a learning topic is also illustrated by this example. To solve each problem, the learner must scan the selected learning resource in a productive way. Narrowing the learning focus is essential to productivity. If learners decide to use the program reference manuals to aid in solving a file-saving problem, they will be more productive to the extent that the manual's index is used to find only the information on file saving. Greater productivity will accrue to learners who narrow the focus further by limiting their reading to the information on file saving that matches the problem situation.

All the learning in this activity is enhanced by discussing the methods and results achieved, after everyone is finished. Strategies used can be compared to those of others. The time invested in each strategy can be compared with its results, allowing for better selections next time. Finally, students can discuss how this activity and their approaches will apply to their on-the-job problem solving.

Collaborative Learning. Work today has become more collaborative. People work in teams. People meet to solve problems. We even work at learning together as we take on the constantly changing tools, techniques, and challenges of modern work. To work in groups, we must be able to learn in groups. Such collaborative learning requires communication skills, observation and reflection skills, and planning and consensus skills. To develop these skills, workers practice them while doing real work. However, as business moves toward more productive work groups, one key is the learning strategies each participant brings to the group. For example, a more productive work group will learn to assess its progress as a group as well as its progress on the task. Group process and group development content can be studied. Once all members of a team know it is normal for groups to progress through stages of group development, discouragement about ups and downs will be mitigated. Once all members of a team learn to listen for both facts and feelings in others, each member will feel more fully heard. Also, once members of a team learn to look back over a meeting and identify how it could have been improved through changes in their behavior, team meetings will improve. Thus, the study of how to be a more productive team provides the content and the processes to be tried out in the work group. Individual and group behavior will be altered by the learning, and the learning experiences add to the group's shared experiences. In addition, learning strategies associated with creating a safe and secure environment will be vital to the ongoing trust level of such work groups.

Conclusion

Instructors need to consciously incorporate learning how to learn in all teaching plans. Adults are individual learners with unique needs. Using learning-how-to-learn techniques is one more way to acknowledge learners' individual differences. In addition, incorporating learning how to learn into our teaching tells adult students that the teachers are realists, because it acknowledges that most student learning is done without teachers. In learning how to learn, adults' learning repertoire is augmented. Each increment of learning strategy offered to students increases their ability to learn wherever they are. No lesson could be more important.

As instructors build learning how to learn into every course, they inevitably shift their role from that of content expert and source of all knowledge to that of co-learner, resource person, and coach (Merriam and Caffarella,

1991). A coach shares methods, approaches, and strategies for learning—the game plan—as well as the specific plays. While expert knowledge (the specific plays) is still of great value, the coaching is what makes it possible for learners to go out and play the game successfully, learning throughout their lifetimes.

References

Argyris, C. "Teaching Smart People How to Learn." *Harvard Business Review,* 1991, *69* (3), 99–109.

Bunker, K. "Leaders and the Dark Chasm of Learning." *Issues and Observations,* 1989, *9* (3), 1, 5–6.

Cunningham, P. M. "Helping Students Extract Meaning from Experience." In R. M. Smith (ed.), *Helping Adults Learn How to Learn.* New Directions for Continuing Education, no.19. San Francisco: Jossey-Bass, 1983.

Gibbons, M. "A Working Model of the Learning-How-to-Learn Process." In R. M. Smith and Associates, *Learning to Learn Across the Life Span.* San Francisco: Jossey-Bass, 1990.

Hammond, D. "Designing and Facilitating Learning-to-Learn Activities." In R. M. Smith and Associates, *Learning to Learn Across the Life Span.* San Francisco: Jossey-Bass, 1990.

Klauer, K. J. "Teaching for Learning-to-Learn: A Critical Appraisal with Some Proposals." Paper presented at the annual meeting of the Educational Research Association, New Orleans, Apr. 1988. (ED 293 861)

Merriam, S. B., and Caffarella, R. S. *Learning in Adulthood: A Comprehensive Guide.* San Francisco: Jossey-Bass, 1991.

Smith, R. M. *Learning How to Learn: Applied Theory for Adults.* Chicago: Follett, 1982.

Smith, R. M. "The Learning-How-to-Learn Concept: Implications and Issues." In R. M. Smith (ed.), *Helping Adults Learn How to Learn.* New Directions for Continuing Education, no. 19. San Francisco: Jossey-Bass, 1983.

Smith, R. M. "Disseminating Current Knowledge About Learning to Learn." In R. M. Smith and Associates, *Learning to Learn Across the Life Span.* San Francisco: Jossey-Bass, 1990a.

Smith, R. M. "The Promise of Learning to Learn." In R. M. Smith and Associates, *Learning to Learn Across the Life Span.* San Francisco: Jossey-Bass, 1990b.

CATHERINE A. STOUCH is an educational and business consultant who works with businesses in eastern Pennsylvania.

Adult learners are confronting learning situations that require new ways of thinking and new approaches to problem solving. Adult and continuing educators can draw on cognitive learning theory to cope with these uncertain learning situations.

Cognitive Apprenticeship Approach to Helping Adults Learn

Barbara LeGrand Brandt, James A. Farmer, Jr., Annette Buckmaster

According to Handy (1990, pp. 5–6), "We are now entering an 'age of unreason', when the future in many areas will be shaped by and for us. It is a time when the only prediction that will hold true is that no predictions will hold true; a time for bold imaginings, thinking the unlikely, and doing the unreasonable." In other words, adults will need to deal with ill-defined, complex, and risky situations. It will be futile to try to simplify them so that ready-made solutions can be applied to them, solutions that were developed for better-defined, less complex, and less risky situations encountered in earlier, more stable times. As Handy observes, we need to better understand the changes that occur around us in order that we as individuals and as a society will suffer less and profit more. He notes that *change* is another word for *growth*, another synonym for *learning* (p. 5).

Adult and continuing educators must draw on cognitive learning theory to confront these uncertain learning situations. One approach, cognitive apprenticeship, is an instructional method for teaching an acceptable way of understanding and doing tasks, solving problems, and dealing with problematic situations (Collins, Brown, and Newman, 1989). It is a useful supplement to traditional types of instruction and self-directed learning experiences. Cognitive apprenticeship is a vehicle for tapping the knowledge and experience of adults who have found ways to effectively handle the tasks, problems, and problematic situations in the current era. It may be difficult and potentially dangerous for learners to try to figure out what to do independently; cognitive apprenticeship can also help them avoid reinventing the wheel. In evaluations of cognitive apprenticeship experiences, learners say this type of learning experience expands their awareness of the factors that should be considered; helps them organize and pay attention to their thought processes while handling difficult tasks, problems, and problematic situations; and emphasizes the importance of particular aspects of such tasks, problems, and problematic situations previously ignored or regarded as unimportant.

Use of Cognitive Apprenticeship

Cognitive apprenticeship can be used whenever someone who can perform the task to be learned can model it acceptably in real life; learners can then be helped to try what has been modeled under protected conditions with coaching. Cognitive apprenticeship may be appropriate when some or all of the following preconditions exist: (1) Learners need to be able to do a task or handle a problem or situation before they encounter it in the real world. (2) There is a realistic, low tolerance for error or risk. (3) Learners have failed to learn adequately through other methods.

Description of Cognitive Apprenticeship

Cognitive apprenticeship is an instructional method for teaching an acceptable way of understanding and dealing with specific types of tasks, problems, or problematic situations. Instructional methods can be used to achieve many different goals. Table 7.1 contrasts what is with what is not the goal of cognitive apprenticeship.

As shown in Table 7.2, cognitive apprenticeship consists of five phases with distinct roles for the models and learners. These are described in more detail later, and each is clarified with an example from continuing pharmacy education. To illustrate the use of cognitive apprenticeship, we begin by presenting a problem situation from the same field.

Problem situation. Community pharmacists are confronted with a significant professional role shift because of required changes in Medicaid reimbursement and new mandatory patient counseling regulations in many states. They are required to shift their primary focus from dispensing medications to focusing on the patient outcomes achieved by using specific drug therapies. Pharmacists should move from behind the counter to working more directly with patients and interacting with other health professionals. In addition, when presented with a Medicaid prescription for an inappropriate dosage, use, or type of medication, pharmacists are required to question the prescriber or even refuse to fill it. For many community pharmacists, these changes are at best uncomfortable; for some, they present an uncertain future. Pharmacists are seeking continuing education programs to learn how to counsel patients and conduct drug utilization reviews of medication therapy.

Phase 1: Modeling. At the heart of cognitive apprenticeship is the *modeling* of an activity that learners need to be able to perform acceptably in the real world. This modeling combines behavioral modeling (Bandura, 1977; Perry

Table 7.1. Goals of Cognitive Apprenticeship

The goal IS to help individuals learn:	The goal is NOT to:
What works acceptably	Give learners opportunities to figure out on their own what will work acceptably
How to understand and deal with specific types of tasks, problems, or situations	Teach unsituated knowledge and principles
The use of appropriately integrated practical and theoretical knowledge	Teach theoretical and practical knowledge in isolation from each other
Acceptable performance	Teach simplified skills that foster novice performance

Table 7.2. Cognitive Apprenticeship Phases

	Role of Model	Role of Learner	Key Concepts
Phase 1: Modeling	Model real-life activity that learner wants to perform satisfactorily. Model states aloud the essence of the activity. He or she can include tricks of the trade.	Observe performance of total activity, not merely the individual steps. Develop a mental model of what the real thing looks like.	Articulation Domain-specific heuristics
Phase 2: Approximating	Providing coaching to the learner. Provide support when needed.	Approximate doing the real thing and articulate its essence. Reflect on the model's performance. Use self-monitoring and self-correction.	Scaffolding Coaching
Phase 3: Fading	Decrease coaching and scaffolding.	Continue to approximate the real thing. Operate in increasingly complex, risky, or ill-defined situations. Work individually or in groups.	Fading
Phase 4: Self-directed learning	Provide assistance only when requested.	Practice doing the real thing alone. Do so within specified limits acceptable to profession and society.	Self-directed learning
Phase 5: Generalizing	Discuss the generalizability of what has been learned.	Discuss the generalizability of what has been learned.	Generalizability

and Furukawa, 1977) and cognitive modeling (Meichenbaum, 1977; Gist, 1989). The model must be someone who can perform the activity acceptably in the real world. The behavioral modeling consists of a live demonstration of how to do something, or, if necessary, the demonstration can be presented on videotape. It is essential that learners observe the model performing the entire activity rather than parts of the activity or subskills. This enables them to develop a mental model of what doing the real thing looks like.

During or immediately after the behavioral modeling, cognitive modeling occurs. In cognitive modeling, models state aloud (or *articulate*) the essence of their thinking. This may include a description of the tricks or strategies that help one do the real thing. Some of these strategies are helpful in many situations; some can only be applied to particular situations.

> After the prerequisite classroom instruction about interviewing a patient, a learner (Bill) and a clinical pharmacy professor (Susan) work in an outpatient pharmacy. Susan models how to interview a patient to seek relevant information about potential drug-related problems. Once the patient has left, she explains what a pharmacist must remember in order to conduct a thorough patient interview and review of a computer patient profile. She discusses the language she used in alerting the patient to possible food-drug interactions. She demonstrates the tricks of the trade used to handle common problems safely.

Phase 2: Approximating. After observing the modeling, learners *approximate* doing the real thing and articulate the essence of their thoughts. In most cognitive apprenticeship experiences, there are three kinds of learner articulation, which occur at different times. Prior to the activity, learners articulate what they plan to do and why. During the activity, they articulate thoughts about the process (unless this interferes with the activity). After the activity, they reflect on and articulate the differences between their performance and the model's performance. The learners' articulation enables the model to monitor their intended performance and provide assistance as necessary. Articulation also helps learners develop self-monitoring and self-correction skills. Reflection is facilitated by discussion, alternation of model and learner activities, and learner problem solving under guidance.

Learners' efforts to do the real thing are *scaffolded* to minimize risks and provide support as needed. Scaffolding consists of physical aids and the model's assistance with difficult parts of the activity. This scaffolding permits learners to approximate doing the real thing as much as possible. The model *coaches* the learners, supplying feedback about their performance and suggesting improvements. Remediation is provided as necessary, based on the learners' difficulties in the scaffolded performance.

> Bill approximates Susan's behavior, articulating thoughts that occur during the process. Bill's efforts are scaffolded initially by using actors who simu-

late patients. Susan coaches Bill, offering suggestions about how to improve performance. Susan provides remediation if errors in Bill's articulation suggest faulty thinking. Susan encourages Bill to reflect by asking Bill to contrast his own performance with what he has seen modeled in the outpatient pharmacy.

Phase 3: Fading. Learners, individually or in groups (through *cooperative learning*) (Johnson and Johnson, 1987), continue to approximate doing the real thing. Coaching and scaffolding decrease (the *fading* process) as learners demonstrate increased ability to do the real thing.

When Bill's performance with the simulated patients warrants, Bill and Susan move to the outpatient pharmacy. Initially Bill is assigned patients with less complex pharmaceutical problems, learning how to counsel them on their medications. Susan can take over the interview if Bill gets into trouble. This is a continuation of scaffolding in the real world. As Bill's demonstrated ability to counsel patients increases, Susan's monitoring and assistance fade.

Phase 4: Self-Directed Learning. This *internalizing* phase starts when learners are able to approximate doing the real thing satisfactorily, sometimes only after a series of successive approximations. In this phase, they practice doing the real thing on their own (*self-directed learning*), in their own ways, within specified acceptable limits. Assistance is provided by the instructor or model only at the learner's request.

Bill returns to his own community pharmacy. He is encouraged to call Susan and participate in weekly teleconferences so that she can assist if necessary. Internalization occurs as Bill engages in self-directed learning under a variety of conditions, adapting within acceptable limits what he has learned from the model.

Phase 5: Generalizing. The model and learners discuss the *generalizability* of what has been learned. The discussion can serve as an advance organizer (West, Farmer, and Wolff, 1991), relating what has been learned in the cognitive apprenticeship experience to subsequent learning. Without the fifth phase, cognitive apprenticeship—with its emphasis on learning how to understand and deal acceptably with a particular type of task, problem, or situation—would be very limiting (Resnick, 1987). This phase helps ensure that learners will appropriately generalize the learning achieved to other similar tasks and problems.

Susan and Bill discuss the generalizability of what Bill has learned and its implications for further instruction. They identify other situations where what has been learned can be applied and consider the next steps in learning pharmacy practice.

Additional Example of Cognitive Apprenticeship: Use of TQM Principles in Project Management

The following example of cognitive apprenticeship illustrates different aspects of this type of instruction.

Problem situation. Because of changes in international and national situations, project managers (PMs) are faced with lower budgets, decreases in personnel, and increased scrutiny of their projects. To improve the way their offices function under these pressures, many PMs are instituting total quality management (TQM) practices. This cognitive apprenticeship experience is designed to help PM professionals learn to function in TQM teams to solve typical complex and risky project management problems. Vice President G., who has been using TQM for the past two years, is the model. A series of scenarios, each focusing on a specific type of management problem, are used to show how teams deal with these kinds of problems. For each scenario, learners receive a handout that describes the information a manager will typically have available.

Phase 1. In the first scenario, Vice President G. *models* his use of teams in the development of new programs. He *articulates* the pros and cons of various approaches and the ways he communicates with the teams, building support for various ideas. The problems typically encountered and strategies learned for thinking about how to handle them are discussed.

Phase 2. The learners form teams, assuming various manager roles, and they approximate what Vice President G. modeled as they work on a particular project development problem. Each team member is given specific information about the problem and information about how it affects people in this particular role. Vice President G. and assistants from his office *coach* the learner teams, providing suggestions, as necessary, on how to proceed. Learners' efforts are *scaffolded* with checklists of possible factors to consider. Each learner is asked to make up a list of the most important factors to keep in mind and of what to do about each one. This process encourages *reflection*, which helps learners evaluate their skills. Vice President G. and his assistants provide remediation in the form of suggestions about how to change faulty approaches, as necessary.

Phase 3. The learners are given more difficult problems and new team assignments. Vice President G. and his assistants offer help as needed. As the teams increase in proficiency, this guidance *fades.*

Phase 4. The learners individually develop their own plans for using a team to deal with a complex problem drawn from the real world. Vice President G. provides assistance only on request.

Phase 4 (alternate). The learners move into management positions, where they work in TQM teams on real problems. They turn to Vice President G. and his assistants for help when they need it.

Phase 5. The learners meet with Vice President G. (or talk with him in a conference call). They discuss the *generalizability* of what was learned. He tells them about other ways he has used his team-building strategies. They share their experiences and discuss the implications of what they have learned in phase 4.

The Power of Cognitive Apprenticeship

Most adult learners and instructors are likely to have experienced the power of cognitive apprenticeship as an instructional tool sometime during their lives. Cognitive apprenticeship derives its power from knowledgeable, proficient people showing learners how to do something and stating aloud what they are thinking while doing the activity. They present the task in a realistic context. The key is that what is shown and explained is the real thing, combining the what, how, when, and why. It is the main method used to teach people how to perform tasks that contain elements of basic physical (or motor) skills, thinking (cognitive) skills, problem-solving skills, or integrative skills. Familiar examples include such diverse activities as driver education, flight training, and sports training.

The key to cognitive apprenticeship is that models demonstrate and explain how they deal with ill-defined, complex, and risky problems and give the learners an opportunity to approximate this behavior under risk-controlled conditions. Cognitive apprenticeship does not seek to develop competencies, although they may result from its use. Rather, it seeks to help individuals learn to do particular types of tasks and solve specific types of problems or problematic situations competently. Cognitive apprenticeship provides access to knowledge that traditional forms of instruction cannot offer. This is knowledge normally held tacitly about how to perform in the real world. By asking people with real-world experience to state their thoughts aloud, much tacit knowledge is made explicit.

Learners from a wide range of backgrounds can benefit from participation in cognitive apprenticeship experiences. Those with little or no real-life experience do not have to learn to handle challenging situations on their own. Through cognitive apprenticeship experiences, they can learn how others cope with such difficulties. Learners who have a great deal of experience can also benefit from cognitive apprenticeships, since they can be taught by models who are experts.

Planning and Implementing Cognitive Apprenticeship Experiences

To make cognitive apprenticeships work well, care must be taken in selecting the type of task, problem, or problematic situation; arranging for modeling with articulation; providing coaching; and arranging scaffolding. Suggestions for doing this are presented below.

Select a particular type of real-world task, problem, or problematic situation. The task, problem, or problematic situation can range from well-defined to ill-defined alternatives and from entailing little or no risk to considerable risk in a specific situation. It should be an important one that learners frequently encounter in the real world. Cognitive apprenticeship is particularly helpful in dealing with ill-defined, complex, and risky problems.

Arrange for modeling. Who can model? The model must fully understand the what, how, when, and why of the activity to be modeled and must perform it in an acceptable way in the real world. Cognitive apprenticeship can involve one model helping a single student or a small group of students learn to do something acceptably. It can also entail one model interacting with a large group of students, who all observe the modeling and hear the demonstrator's articulation. Efficient and effective cognitive apprenticeship experiences with one model and 100 students have been conducted.

Multiple models can be helpful in showing learners a variety of effective approaches. The opportunity to identify the models' strengths and weaknesses and compare them with the learners' own can help learners select the approaches that best fit their abilities.

When there are large numbers of students, they can be formed into groups for phase 2 and phase 3 activities. The group members can be coached and scaffolded together. A promising approach is to first use a videotape in which a proficient person models and articulates how to understand and deal with a particular type of problematic situation. Senior students with a great deal of experience can scaffold and coach less experienced students. In phase 5, the learners all meet with the model for a wrap-up session in which they share the lessons they have learned and discuss the generalizability of the lessons.

Models must express the essence of their thoughts, which may otherwise be unspoken, while they demonstrate how to do a particular aspect of the task. The goal should be verbalization of thoughts that occur during performance, descriptions of thought processes, summaries of internal speech and what the subject is sensing, and explanations of the reasons for particular types of thinking (Ericsson and Simon, 1984). Models may not be able to articulate all their thoughts, but learners will still obtain more information about the processes involved this way than they otherwise would. Models may use decision charts, checklists, or flowcharts to help describe their thought processes while performing the action. The spoken thoughts add a dimension to the learning process that is not present in other types of learning experiences. The instructor can encourage verbalization of thoughts by asking models and learners to think aloud while they perform, if this does not interfere with performance. Asking first for descriptions and then for explanations helps models to "tell it like it is" instead of "telling it like it ought to be."

Provide coaching. Coaching involves observing and helping learners while they attempt to do the task to be learned. It includes directing learners' attention; reminding them about steps overlooked; giving hints and feedback; and providing additional tasks, problems, or problematic situations as needed for demonstration and practice purposes.

In coaching, models typically explain the what of the activity in terms learners can understand and can relate to their background knowledge, with clear reminders or additional directions about how, when, and why to proceed. The models also identify "bugs" in learners' thinking and help correct them. Bugs are not the same as faults or failures but are errors made when trying to understand or interpret experiences. Bugs may result from learners' attempts to simplify the real thing. Following is an example of a bug in a community pharmacy situation: Instead of seeking the necessary verification, a pharmacist jumps to conclusions about a patient's diagnosis because of the prescription presented at the pharmacy and incorrectly counsels the patient about use of the medication.

Arrange for scaffolding. This involves providing support and regulating task difficulty so that the level of challenge is optimal. Learners will succeed only when learning tasks stretch their ability to an appropriate degree. Too little challenge will not encourage maximum learning; too much will foster frustration, discouragement with the learning process, and the development of "buggy" thinking, which may be hard to correct.

The challenge level of the learning environment can be controlled by manipulating task specifications, time and risk factors, or interactions between the various persons involved in the cognitive apprenticeship experience. The learning environment should (1) make it likely that learners will succeed in approximating what was modeled, with coaching and other assistance provided as needed; (2) help them pay attention to critical skills and knowledge; and (3) help learners recognize and overcome buggy thinking.

Conclusion

Cognitive apprenticeship as described above differs markedly from forms of instruction that teach content with the assumption that students will be able to apply it on their own successfully at some time in the future. It is also very different from types of instruction that rely exclusively on self-directed learning, in which learners seek to learn the what, how, when, and why on their own. Because it controls the level of risk and complexity of what is being learned and provides access to tacit knowledge, cognitive apprenticeship is a useful tool for helping adults learn to perform ill-defined, complex, and risky tasks. These tasks are becoming more and more prevalent. In the future, cognitive apprenticeship and other instructional tools like it that promote learning how to learn (see Chapter Six) will play an increasingly crucial role in our society.

References

Bandura, A. *Social Learning Theory*. Englewood Cliffs, N.J.: Prentice Hall, 1977.

Collins, A., Brown, J. S., and Newman, S. E. "Cognitive Apprenticeship: Teaching the Crafts of Reading, Writing, and Mathematics." In L. B. Resnick (ed.), *Knowing, Learning, and Instruction: Essays in Honor of Robert Glaser*. Hillsdale, N.J.: Erlbaum, 1989.

Ericsson, K., and Simon, H. *Protocol Analysis: Verbal Reports as Data*. Cambridge, Mass.: MIT Press, 1984.

Gist, M. "The Influence of Training Method on Self-Efficacy and Idea Generation Among Managers." *Personnel Psychology*, 1989, *42*, 787–803.

Handy, C. *The Age of Unreason*. Boston: Harvard Business School Press, 1990.

Johnson, D. W., and Johnson, R. T. *Learning Together and Alone: Cooperation, Competition, and Individualistic Learning*. Englewood Cliffs, N.J.: Prentice Hall, 1987.

Meichenbaum, D. *Cognitive Behavior Modification*. New York: Plenum, 1977.

Perry, M. A., and Furukawa, M. J. "Modeling Methods." In F. K. Kanfer and A. P. Goldstein (eds.), *Helping People Change: A Textbook of Methods*. (2nd ed.) Elmsford, N.Y.: Pergamon Press, 1977.

Resnick, L. B. "Learning in School and Out." *Educational Researcher*, Dec. 1987, pp. 13–20.

West, C. K., Farmer, J. A., and Wolff, P. M. *Instructional Design: Implications from Cognitive Science*. Englewood Cliffs, N.J.: Prentice Hall, 1991.

BARBARA LEGRAND BRANDT is associate director of continuing pharmacy education at the College of Pharmacy, University of Kentucky, Lexington.

JAMES A. FARMER, JR., is professor of continuing education, University of Illinois, Urbana-Champaign.

ANNETTE BUCKMASTER is a consultant to the Office of Continuing Education, Training and Development, University of Illinois, Urbana-Champaign.

This chapter summarizes aspects important for the promotion of successful learning for adults and offers suggestions for promoting further understanding of cognitive learning theory.

A Thematic Summary and Future Directions for Understanding Adults as Learners

Daniele D. Flannery

As promised, this sourcebook has provided an overview of cognitive theory and its contribution to adult education. Its purpose has been to introduce basic cognitive functioning and its implications for adult learning. In so doing, three major themes emerged.

First, learners vary in the cognitive learning strategies they bring to the teaching-learning exchange. These strategies may be based on people's cognitive learning styles, that is, the characteristic ways they perceive, process, store, and retrieve information. In this sourcebook, attention was given to two aspects of cognitive styles: perceptual modalities (Chapter One) and analytical and global processing (Chapter Two). The way memory works was presented in Chapter Four, with attention given to the connection between people's cognitive learning styles of analytical, global, and perceptual modalities and their styles of storing and retrieving information.

Often the cognitive learning strategies people bring to the teaching-learning exchange are not their personal cognitive learning styles. Rather, they are those strategies that learners have acquired, by habit or intentionally, to meet the needs of the teacher, the subject matter, and the classroom structure.

The second theme of this sourcebook is that the cognitive learning strategies people bring to the teaching-learning exchange may or may not result in successful learning. The issue here is not whether the learner can learn, but whether the cognitive strategies being employed for learning are appropriate. Learners may employ strategies that do not work in all, most, or particular settings. These strategies may be the result of learners not understanding their own learning styles (see Chapter Five) and the connection between these styles and the teaching-learning exchange. They may be the result of ineffective learning habits. They may be the result of the learner not having learned the skills of how to learn (see Chapter Six).

The third theme of this sourcebook is that instructors, facilitators, and tutors must attend to the issue of learning strategies in order to facilitate successful learning. Cognitive learning strategies that work for learners must be ascertained. Affective dimensions (see Chapter Three) of personality such as needs for structure, levels of anxiety, and locus of control, because they are involved in every aspect of cognitive learning, must be attended to. In new learning situations, cognitive strategies must be modeled and taught (Chapter Seven). Finally, adult educators must analyze and acknowledge the ways in which their teaching, the texts used, and the testing structures and learning structures of the institution or classroom promote certain kinds of cognitive learning over others. If successful learning is to be promoted, these teaching structures and settings must be critically reviewed and consciously kept or changed based on the criteria of promoting successful learning for adults.

Before concluding this chapter, it must be noted that in this sourcebook, aspects of the social influences on learning were acknowledged but not stressed. This choice was deliberate in an effort to concentrate on a manageable amount of data. However, we should acknowledge that cognitive learning has been covered without dealing with the contexts in which learning occurs, the cultural contexts that influence learning, and the inseparability of neurological and social cognition. A future sourcebook is called for that will stress the social aspects of learning and the integration of social cognition with internal neurological cognition. All learning involves the integration of the individual and the social.

In particular, I suggest two topics for future explication. The first is how learning occurs in particular settings. Such an undertaking would concentrate both on the interactive construction of learning itself and on the context in which the learning is situated. This exploration was begun by Brandt, Farmer, and Buckmaster's consideration of cognitive apprenticeship in Chapter Seven of this volume. Others who are studying cognition as socially defined include Lave (1988), Resnick (1987), Rogoff and Lave (1984), Schön (1983), and West, Farmer, and Wolff (1991).

The second area that needs explication is that of cultural learning styles. The way people communicate, express values, think, learn, and relate to others is a product of the value system and other attributes of their home, community, and culture. People from varying cultures may have different ways of thinking and learning. These cultural learning differences can be called *cultural learning styles* (Flannery, 1992). In cognitive processing, for example, women, African Americans, Mexican Americans, and Puerto-Rican Americans tend to display the patterns of global learners (Flannery, 1991, 1992; Shaw, 1993; Ramirez, 1982; Ramirez and Casteneda, 1974). Further, unlike those of Anglo-Americans, African Americans' ways of knowing demonstrate the integration of the cognitive and affective domains (Shaw, 1993; Hunt, 1974; Dixon, 1976). The interrelatedness of culture and learning has been neglected for too long in our study of learning. Clearly, culture influences learning style as well as subtle aspects of perception, cognition, and affect. In addition to the sources just cited, further discussion of the connection between culture and learning is provided by Conti and Fellenz (1988), Diaz-Lefebve (1990), Hvitfeldt (1986), Marashio (1982), Ogbu (1978), and Pratt (1988).

In closing, I hope that practitioners will increasingly conceive of learning not as an isolated ladder with progressive rungs to climb, but as a lattice with horizontal and vertical connections and interweavings. Just as the cognitive and affective domains are interwoven, so too are neurological and social cognition integral parts of the same lattice.

References

Conti, G. J., and Fellenz, R. A. "Teaching and Learning Styles and the Native American Learner." In C. E. Warren (ed.), *Proceedings of the 29th Adult Education Research Conference*. Calgary, Canada, 1988.

Diaz-Lefebve, R. "The Hispanic Adult Learner in a Rural Community College." In B. Cassara (ed.), *Adult Education in a Multicultural Society*. New York: Routledge, 1990.

Dixon, V. J. "World Views and Research Methodology." In L. King (ed.), *African Philosophy: Assumptions and Paradigms on Black Persons*. Los Angeles: Fanon Center, 1976.

Flannery, D. D. "Adult Education: Little Boxes All the Same?" *Adult Learning*, 1991, *3* (3), 31.

Flannery, D. D. "Towards an Understanding and Implementation of Culturally Diverse Learning Styles." *Community Education Journal*, 1992, *19* (4), 10–12.

Hunt, D. "Reflections on Racial Perspectives." *Journal of Afro-American Issues*, 1974, *2*, 363–367.

Hvitfeldt, C. "Traditional Culture, Perceptual Style, and Learning: The Classroom Behavior of Hmong Adults." *Adult Education Quarterly*, 1986, *36* (2), 65–77.

Lave, J. *Cognition in Practice: Mind, Mathematics and Culture in Everyday Life*. Cambridge, England: Cambridge University Press, 1988.

Marashio, P. "Enlighten My Mind . . . Examining the Learning Process Through Native Americans' Ways." *Journal of American Indian Education*, Feb. 1982, pp. 2–10.

Ogbu, J. *Minority Education and Caste: The American System in Cross-Cultural Perspective*. San Diego, Calif.: Academic Press, 1978.

Pratt, P. "Cross-Cultural Relevance of Selected Psychological Perspectives on Learning." In M. Zukas (ed.), *Proceedings of Transatlantic Dialogue: A Research Exchange*. Leeds, England: University of Leeds, 1988.

Ramirez, M., III. "Cognitive Styles and Cultural Diversity." Paper presented at the annual meeting of the American Educational Research Association, New York, Mar. 1982. (ED 218 380)

Ramirez, M., and Castenada, A. *Cultural Democracy, Bicognitive Development, and Education*. San Diego, Calif.: Academic Press, 1974.

Resnick, L. B. "Learning in School and Out." *Educational Researcher*, 1987, *16* (9), 13–20.

Rogoff, B., and Lave, L. (eds.). *Everyday Cognition: Its Development in Social Context*. Cambridge, Mass.: Harvard University Press, 1984.

Schön, D. *The Reflective Practitioner*. New York: Basic Books, 1983.

Shaw, M. "African-American Learning-to-Learn-to-Live in Response to Diseducation: A Phe-
nomenological Investigation." In D. D. Flannery (ed.), *Proceedings of the 34th Annual Adult
Education Research Conference*. University Park: The Pennsylvania State University, 1993.
West, C. K., Farmer, J. A., and Wolff, P. M. *Instructional Design: Implications from Cognitive Science*. Englewood Cliffs, N.J.: Prentice Hall, 1991.

DANIELE D. FLANNERY *is assistant professor of adult education and coordinator of
the adult education Doctor of Education program at The Pennsylvania State University, Harrisburg.*

INDEX

Adult education, affective domain in, 27–29

Affective domain: in adult education, 27–29; as dimension of learning style, 48; and education, 25; and instructional design, 31–32; and Pierce-Gray classification model, 30–31; and taxonomy of educational objectives, 29–30; and triune brain, 26–27

Aging, and memory, 37–38

Analytical information processing, 15–17, 23; identifying, 18–19; teaching for, 19–23. *See also* Learning styles

Anderson, J., 41

Approximating, in cognitive apprenticeship, 71, 72–73

Argyris, C., 61

Atkinson, R., 35

Atkinson-Shiffrin model of memory, 35–36, 44

Attention, and memory, 36, 38, 39, 45

Automaticity, 39

Babich, A. M., 54

Baddeley, A., 35, 37, 44

Bahrick, H., 37

Bamberg, M., 37

Bandler, R., 8

Bandura, A., 70

Barbe, W. B., 6, 7, 8, 53

Barbe-Milone Modality Checklist, 52, 53, 55

Bates, M., 53

Bellezza, F., 43

Blank, W. E., 9, 12, 55

Bloom, B., 29, 30

Bloomsburg University, instructional approach at, 9–10

Bolles, E., 43, 44

Bonham, L. A., 54

Bootzin, R., 36

Boss, B., 41

Botwinick, J., 35

Brain: interrelatedness of dimensions of, 29–31; triune, 26–27

Brandt, B. L., 80

Briggs, K. C., 53

Bringman, W., 37

Brookfield, S. D., 12

Brown, J. S., 69

Buckmaster, A., 80

Bunker, K., 61, 65

Buzan, T., 20

Caffarella, R. S., 35, 38, 64, 65, 66

Caine, G., 27, 32

Caine, R. N., 27, 32

Canfield, A. A., 53

Canfield's Learning Styles Inventory, 52, 53

Casteneda, A., 81

Cawley, R. W., 15

Center for Innovative Teaching Experiences (CITE) Learning Styles Instrument, 52, 54, 55

Cercy, S. P., 53

Cherry, C. E., Jr., 53

Chunking, 40, 45

Coaching, in cognitive apprenticeship, 71, 72–73, 74, 77

Cognitive apprenticeship, 69–70, 77; examples of, 70, 72–75; goals of, 71; phases of, 71; planning and implementing, 75–77; power of, 75; use of, 70

Cognitive learning strategies, 79–80

Cognitive style, 1, 47

Cognitive Style Mapping, 52, 54

Cohen, R. A., 16

Collaborative learning, 66

Collins, A., 69

Conti, G. J., 81

Controlled processes, 39

Coolidge-Parker, J., 55

Cox, P. W., 15, 16

Craik, F., 35, 37

Cranston, M., 15

Cultural learning styles, 80–81

Cunningham, P. M., 63

Curriculum development, affective domain in, 28–29

Daloz, L. A., 29

Das, J. P., 1

Ordering Information

New Directions for Adult and Continuing Education is a series of paperback books that explores issues of common interest to instructors, administrators, counselors, and policy makers in a broad range of adult and continuing education settings—such as colleges and universities, extension programs, businesses, the military, prisons, libraries, and museums. Books in the series are published quarterly in spring, summer, fall, and winter and are available for purchase by subscription and individually.

Subscriptions for 1993 cost $47.00 for individuals (a savings of 25 percent over single-copy prices) and $62.00 for institutions, agencies, and libraries. Please do not send institutional checks for personal subscriptions. Standing orders are accepted.

Single copies cost $15.95 when payment accompanies order. (California, New Jersey, New York, and Washington, D.C., residents please include appropriate sales tax.) Billed orders will be charged postage and handling.

Discounts for quantity orders are available. Please write to the address below for information.

All orders must include either the name of an individual or an official purchase order number. Please submit your order as follows:
    Subscriptions: specify series and year subscription is to begin
    Single copies: include individual title code (such as CE1)

Mail all orders to:
    Jossey-Bass Publishers
    350 Sansome Street
    San Francisco, California 94104

For single-copy sales outside of the United States contact:
    Maxwell Macmillan International Publishing Group
    866 Third Avenue
    New York, New York 10022

For subscription sales outside of the United States, contact any international subscription agency or Jossey-Bass directly.

OTHER TITLES AVAILABLE IN THE
NEW DIRECTIONS FOR ADULT AND CONTINUING EDUCATION SERIES
Ralph G. Brockett, Editor-in-Chief
Alan B. Knox, Consulting Editor